Letters From Lines And Spaces
by
Terry Johns

LETTERS, LINES AND SPACES

With gratitude to Robert Hamilton for his patience and diligence without which this would not have been possible. TJ

LETTERS, LINES AND SPACES

"Letters from Lines and Spaces"

A colourful, humorous, and sometimes perplexing picture of British musical life, written by a musician with a distinguished career that spans forty five years in classical and popular music, recalling his early experiences in orchestras with Benjamin Britten, Leopold Stokowski and Leonard Bernstein, in pop music, with Deep Purple, Frank Zappa, Barry White, and Paul McCartney, and as a top "session" french horn player featured on many studio recordings and television shows with Peggy Lee, Barbara Streisand, Paul Simon, and Tony Bennett.

Terry Johns played on dozens of film sound tracks, including "Fiddler on the roof", "Oliver", "Battle of Britain", "Diamonds are for ever" and "Star Wars".

The author's musical life began in the brass band of Tower Colliery in South Wales, where his father worked as a miner. These letters are a personal tale of celebration and survival in the sometimes hostile and uncertain environment of professional music, where often the only security of employment is one's skill and ability, and difficulties are greeted with the humour and resilience that has always characterized working musicians everywhere.

They are an important chronicle of a generation of players who, as well as experiencing the golden era that saw London as the musical capital of the world, encountered the difficult challenges of the technological age, the acrimonious strike against the BBC in 1980, the diminishing of their union's power, the digital revolution, and the decline of the recording industry.

LETTERS, LINES AND SPACES

"The life of a musician is a privilege" - Alice Hertz Sommer.

MY MUSICAL LIFE BEGAN IN THE VALLEYS OF SOUTH WALES, WHERE OUR LOCAL POSTMAN GAVE PIANO LESSONS IN THE EVENINGS, FOR FIVE SHILLINGS, AND THE TOWER COLLIERY WHERE MY FATHER WORKED, HAD A BRASS BAND THAT PRACTICED IN AN ENGINE SHED. ONCE OR TWICE I HAD DREAMED, WILDLY, OF BEING A PROFESSIONAL PLAYER.

MY BOYHOOD DREAMS HAD NOT BEEN WILD ENOUGH!

Dear Mr. Evans

I'm waiting to be taken to Carnegie Hall for our second concert in New York. The whole of the city is wrapped in snow now, and glittering with Christmas lights. Outside our hotel, horse-drawn carriages wait in a line to trot the tourists around Central Park, and the bellboys in their purple and gold livery are hurrying across the soft carpets under the chandeliers. I feel as if I'm in a film!

'The Royal Philharmonic is magnificent' said the New York Times this morning. They really are too, and I'm a part of it now, which is hardly believable, because they're so nonchalant about it all, having been here so many times before, and I feel just as if I'm running along behind. I can't sleep if we have an early start to make, for fear of missing a train or an aeroplane, so I go out and roam the city streets.

This morning I went to Eddy O'Connor's twenty-four hour diner, where you can be comfortably anonymous, with only the bartender and the empty chairs and tables for company. I sat for a while, with my coffee, contemplating Christmas in Wales, until two city cops came stamping in out of the snow to get a bowl of Irish stew against the cold, and brought me back to reality and the reasons for my being here.

Last night in all my excitement the Beethoven symphony seemed to pass in an instant, leaving me awash with applause and disbelief. My life has changed beyond recognition in these few months just as you said it would, the most astonishing thing about it all being the pace of everything. Before we left London I played as an anxious guest with the London Symphony Orchestra performing Britten's War requiem with Fischer Diskau, Peter Pears, and Britten himself conducting. We played a marathon Wagner concert at the Festival Hall with Leopold Stokowski and Birgit Nilsson, and recorded a Tchaikovsky symphony with Antal Dorati; all that in two weeks! I had no idea what to expect from a life in music, even after all you had told me, but the pace of everything is exhausting. Tomorrow we'll play in Baltimore and on Saturday, Philadelphia.

The audiences in America are full of enthusiasm and they applaud and cheer like anything. After our concerts people wait in the street to talk to us and some of them imagine that we all know the Queen personally, and live in Buckingham Palace. My new friend Pat is an Irish violinist, who has been here many times before, and lies to them mischievously with intimate details of the Queen's sumptuous life style and her sordid private life. He tells them that because we play in her orchestra we are all exempt from income tax, and that we borrow her yacht for our holiday trips. --- It's astounding how far he can go, without being found out.

With regard to the music, hardly anyone here reads the reviews in the newspapers, and they don't appear to listen to anything that conductors say to them, but at a performance where they have some freedom to play, the world looks on in wonder.

There is considerable uncertainty about the future of this orchestra, which was all explained to me when I was invited to join, that has to do with the recent death of Sir Thomas Beecham and the fact that neither the Arts Council nor the Royal Philharmonic Society wants the orchestra to continue without him. This has led the players to take over the running of it themselves in the form of their own company, of which I am now, by invitation, a shareholder. The men, by and large don't seem over anxious about their situation though. Most of them say that they've seen it all before and that music in England is always in some sort of crisis.

LETTERS, LINES AND SPACES

I know you'll say this is my old problem of self-confidence, but I can't help feeling that they may have been having some difficulty filling this job that I'm so excited about. Nevertheless it is exciting, and tonight we'll be playing the seventh symphony of Beethoven and Ida Haendel will be playing the Brahms violin concerto. After that we'll go to Jack Dempsey's restaurant and then to the Half Note to hear Sonny Rollins.

I'll be in Wales for Christmas and that's the most exciting thing of all. I'll play carols with Tower band on Christmas morning and at midday there'll be a concert with the choir in the Miner's Club. Can I come and see you on Boxing Day? It's a lovely walk in good weather. I'll bring my father's dog and promise not to talk about myself all the time, but my life has changed so dramatically which is largely due to you, who taught me almost everything I know about music, and for that I'll always be grateful.

It's time to go now out into "subzero" New York. Through the window I can see the snow falling through the trees in the park. I'll go down to the lobby and wait for the transport to the concert. Once again, thank you for all this and please give my best to Mr. Griffiths (English) who taught me to write a letter and that being hopeless at rugby is not such a terrible thing.

Yours ever

Terry Johns

P.S. Before we left for the US I was at Denham studios for a few days playing on the soundtrack for the "Blue Max" starring George Peppard, James Mason and Ursula Andress that comes out next year. Jerry Goldsmith wrote the music with lots of "flying" horn writing for the First World War Luftwaffe story. Playing for films is fascinating. I'll tell you all about it one day.

LETTERS, LINES AND SPACES

BARRY TUCKWELL WAS MY FIRST HORN TEACHER. WHILST I WAS STUDYING AT THE ROYAL ACADEMY, HE WAS THE PRINCIPAL HORN OF THE LONDON SYMPHONY ORCHESTRA, AND CHAIRMAN OF ITS BOARD OF DIRECTORS.

IN BRITAIN, BEFORE THE ESTABLISHMENT OF THE RACE RELATIONS BOARD IN 1966, RACIAL DISCRIMINATION WAS OVERT, WIDESPREAD, AND LEGAL.

33 George Terrace
Primrose Hill

November 1963

Dear Mum and Dad

I took my horn lesson at the Academy yesterday, breathless, after climbing the stairs to a tiny room at the very top of the building that looks over the trees to Regents Park, and Primrose Hill, which is where I live now, albeit temporarily. My teacher seems to be pleased at the standard of my playing, which does bring me great relief after all the time I spent before I came to London, worrying that because I didn't have a proper horn teacher, I might not be doing things in the right way. No one ever mentions brass bands here you know.

On Friday mornings, the Academy orchestra under Sir John Barbirolli fills the whole building with astonishing sounds. All the best choir trainers, conductors and instrumental teachers are here, and the students perform to a really high standard.

Before I came to London I couldn't escape a fear that they would be much better than I was, so it's a relief to know now that I can do as well as most, and to have a teacher at last.

LETTERS, LINES AND SPACES

I will feel even better and able to settle to some work when I find another place to live. Flat hunting means trudging the London streets from one newsagent's window to another, and perusing the postcard advertisements which unappealing task occupied me, and my fellow evictees for most of yesterday. At one point, among the "NO BLACKS OR IRISH", and "EUROPEANS ONLY" provisos, I came across a "NO WELSH" variant that surprised and hurt me until I gave it some thought.

No race on the earth is immune to this of course, and these dirty postcards are just as much about privilege and property as anything else, I am sure.

We answered the "No Welsh" advertisement because the house was very close by the Academy, so when we got to the doorstep, my pals told me to stand back and to keep my mouth shut, but all was lost anyway when we were forced to admit to being music students, so we are homeless still but only temporarily I'm sure.

The Devonshire arms, near Harley St. has a piano and the landlord has asked me to play it on Saturday nights for a fiver. As I already play on most nights but for fun I consider it no great hardship at all.

I'll be home for Christmas, festooned and festive with fivers!

Huge love and homesickness.

Terence

LETTERS, LINES AND SPACES

BERT MERRETT WAS A TROMBONIST AT THE BBC IN WALES AND IN LATER LIFE HE WAS THE BANDMASTER AT HIRWAUN. HE HELPED ME TO BLOW MY FIRST NOTE WHEN I WAS 10 YEARS OLD, AND ENCOURAGED ME TO BECOME A PROFESSIONAL PLAYER.

MERTHYR TYDFIL, UNTIL THE EIGHTEENTH CENTURY HAD BEEN AN AGRICULTURAL VILLAGE IN THE TAFF VALLEY OF SOUTH WALES. BY THE EIGHTEEN FORTIES IT WAS AN INDUSTRIAL TOWN WITH THE HIGHEST MORTALITY RATE OF ANY IN BRITAIN, AND THE LIFE EXPECTANCY OF A WORKING CLASS MALE WAS SEVENTEEN AND A HALF YEARS.

Bert Merret
Tower Colliery Band
c/o The British Legion
HIRWAUN
South Wales

Royal Academy of Music
Marylebone Road
LONDON

14th October 1964

Dear Bert

I'm writing to you from the warmth and friendliness of the students' common room at the Academy, and through the streaming rain on the windows, I can see the old Marylebone church, sheltering under the dripping plane trees. I'm presently homeless along with the four other music students who occupied the flat at Fortune Green Road, the fragile tolerance of our landlord, and the tranquility of West Hampstead having been shattered by a very loud and impromptu trombone recital, given at around six o'clock on Sunday morning by our new Bacchanalian sub-tenant. Our desperate pleas for clemency, on behalf of his youthful exuberance, the eccentricity of genius and even our renewed willingness to pay the rent, were met only with resolute indifference, so here we are, homeless and downcast, in the damp grey London weather. I'm longing for some home comfort and intemperance!

My auntie Queenie, whom you know, was the proprietor and grand dame of the "Golden Lion" in Merthyr, and her private parlour at the back of the pub, was a place where only friends and family were invited to drink, and was famous all over the town for its Saturday night concerts.

The room was filled with murmuring Welsh voices, cigarette smoke, heavy old leather furniture, and a Broadwood piano that stood upright against the back wall, under an ornate mirror from the brewery. Between musical items, trays of beer were passed through a serving hatch in the wall that opened onto the Saturday night mayhem of the public bar.

I was the "official" accompanist for the old colliers and their euphonic renditions of popular songs, while my aunties, Millie, Maisie and Iris, decorating the room with their décolletage, permanent waves, and girlish laughter, lit my cigarettes, between pouring out Worthington and excessive praise for my pianistic fumblings. Then at the end of the night, Queenie would appear in her platinum splendour, with folding money and Players cigarettes for me, and pork pies with pickled cabbage for supper.

I know from my local history studies, that Thomas Carlisle called industrial Merthyr a 'vision of hell", and there is a passage in Trollope that tells of a curate who faints when he is posted there, but for a fourteen-year-old boy taking his first strong drink, amongst adoring aunties, pickles and prurience it was as near to heaven as can be imagined, and at times like these. I long for such celestial comforts.

Here in London, I play the piano on Saturday nights, down the road at the "Devonshire Arms". This pub does most of its trade at lunchtimes, calming the nerves of anxious patients from doctors and dentists surgeries on nearby Harley Street with an atmosphere of gentile affluence, smoked salmon sandwiches with French wine, and pink gin in crystal glasses.

LETTERS, LINES AND SPACES

On Saturdays, the customers are mainly local residents in soft shoes and cardigans, and mellifluous English actors, whose faces are as familiar as my family to me, but who I can never put names to, and no one ever sings of course. It's considered antisocial.

Father often told me that I shouldn't "mess about" with brass instruments, and that perseverance at the piano might one day save me from starvation, so having been rendered homeless by a trombone and gainfully employed by the Devonshire Arms, I should be attentive to his advice in the future.

But try as I might to inspire myself, this metropolitan malaise DOES depress me, and the dirty rain pesters the windows like self-pity, so please forgive my indulgence. I will write again when I have somewhere to sleep and London has become less hostile. Then I'll be able to preoccupy myself with something other than my own irrelevances, and to thank you properly for your innumerable kindnesses to me.

Very best regards to you and Beryl

Terry

PS Can I play in the Christmas concert?   PPS Will you lend me a flugel?

LETTERS, LINES AND SPACES

OFFERS OF EMPLOYMENT CAUSED ME TO BECOME IMPATIENT. PLAYING MUSIC FOR MONEY CAN AFFECT ONE'S EVERYDAY LIFE CONSIDERABLY. IN 1964, I SPENT MY FIRST CHRISTMAS APART FROM THE FAMILY.

Mr. & Mrs. A Johns
11 Baptist Place
HIRWAUN
Glamorganshire

Ham
Richmond

13th January 1965

Dear Mum and Dad

How was Christmas? I felt very uncomfortable at first being away from home, but now that I'm playing professionally, I think it's normal to have to give up one's holidays, evenings and weekends. I'll get used to it. It's worth it, and I have money in the bank for the first time.' Toad of Toad Hall' runs for six weeks at Christmas now, it's just a pity I have to play on Christmas Eve.

I've some exciting news. Harry Blech, the conductor of the London Mozart Players has asked me to join his orchestra as a permanent member. I have done some concerts with them as a free-lance, but they want someone permanent. They are world famous, and they have an Italian tour in the spring to Rome and Milan and a few other places, for which they will pay me five pounds a concert. I've never had so much money. As well as this, Charlie Katz has asked me if I would take on 'Oliver' at the New Theatre on a permanent basis. It's been running for years of course so they have a well-tried deputy system, which would enable me to play with the Mozart Players as well. They would pay me twenty-two pounds for eight performances a week. It's a great show. I want you to come to London and see it. You can stay with Auntie Margaret and Uncle Bob.

I went up to Willesden to see them a few weeks ago and Bob was there. With him being a chef and everything, they always give me a marvellous meal. Roast duck we had, and sort of lemon pudding.

LETTERS, LINES AND SPACES

I hope you're as pleased as I am about all this. I told my horn teacher about it, and he says I should just do it and be grateful, and not worry too much about the Academy. I feel as if I should finish my course there properly, but he says, I mustn't miss this opportunity, and attend the Academy whenever I can. My time there will come to an end in July in any case.

How are Uncle Reg and Dilwyn and Cora? Did Reg manage to give a song without me on the piano? Did you hear the band? I thought about you a lot. On Christmas day, I was with my pal Dave Lawrence. His father has a home for children of broken families on Hayling Island so he kindly took me down there in his car after the Christmas Eve performance.

The children performed a panto on Boxing Day -- 'Jack and the Beanstalk' -- and I was roped in to play in that too!! Great fun. They are a lovely family and I felt so welcome there. I'll be in Wales to see you before I go to Italy in the spring. Tell me when you can come to London.

Love to you both.

Terence

PS   Would you consider getting a telephone?   It doesn't cost much unless you use it a lot.

LETTERS, LINES AND SPACES

THOMAS BEECHAM FOUNDED THE ROYAL PHILHARMONIC ORCHESTRA IN 1946.

AFTER HIS DEATH IN 1961 THE PLAYERS FACED A LONG BATTLE FOR SURVIVAL AND FOR THE RIGHT TO USE THE ROYAL TITLE.

WHEN I JOINED THE ORCHESTRA, THEY HAD BEEN EMBATTLED FOR NEARLY FIVE YEARS, THE FINANCIAL DEFICIT WAS MOUNTING AND THE ELECTED BOARD WAS BEING THREATENED WITH LEGAL ACTION.

Mr. Bert Merret   Baltimore Plaza Hotel
c/o The British Legion
HIRWAUN
Glamorgan
                                                          19th February 1966

Dear Bert

I am now a member of the Royal Philharmonic Orchestra. The chairman of the board gave me the news shortly before we left London. This is great news for me of course, and I am still suffering from shock and disbelief. But circumstances here are not ideal, the orchestra is in fact fighting for its life, and the extent of the orchestra's difficulties is considerable, but the excitement and the privilege of playing in it overrides everything that is uncertain or unpleasant. I hope this letter reaches you before I arrive in Wales on the 23rd. I felt a huge thrill just writing that sentence, and thinking of playing the old carols and drinking Hancock's bitter in the club on Christmas morning. You can tell me how you progressed in the "Daily Herald" contest and I'll tell you all about the fantastic brass players that are in this orchestra. One of the trombonists Evan Watkin told me that he remembered playing with you at the BBC. He is a very great player; one of the great players that define the sound of this great orchestra.

LETTERS, LINES AND SPACES

Beecham knew what he was about it seems to me, and the players that I've met here all revere him enormously. I've not heard one word of criticism of him from anyone, though in general they don't think much of conductors at all. The main resentment comes from the vast amounts of money they get which the company is forced to pay of course, if it is to sell any tickets. I don't think the public in England listens to one orchestra in preference to another but they do imagine that this maestro is better than that one especially if he has a foreign sounding name.

In these straitened circumstances it's not surprising that there is a large amount of cynicism here, although it is expressed mainly in the form of humour. I have a friend Patrick, an Irish fiddler, who says that the famous maestri pose the most danger to us, because they get bored with all the fame and money lavished upon them, and manipulate orchestral budgets and musicians' lives wherever they can, simply to amuse themselves. When I asked him where music featured in all this, he said I was far too fond of music to be doing it for a living, and that if you're addicted to something you can't enjoy it to the full.

Confusion, excitement and extreme elation are the things that define my life at the moment, but I'm certain this can't continue, and as time goes on I'm sure I'll become accustomed to this bizarre life and comfortable with these fascinating people. Gethin Evans told me in my years at school that I should have been a composer but I wouldn't have missed this for anything, and I'm certain that I won't feel so nervous when I'm as familiar with the repertoire as these people are.

I can remember being very nervous at our band contests in Cardiff and Swansea, most especially as we waited for the results, but now I wait for the reviews in the papers and always feel slightly uncomfortable reading them because no one else appears to be interested.

We've recently had notice of a Welsh tour in the spring, which I'm told is a regular event that everybody looks forward to. We'll be performing at all the places I played at with the Welsh Youth Orchestra and Tower Band on those great miners' gala days with the sunlight gleaming on the brass and the union banners. I think I had the range of one octave on the cornet when I was eleven and I can remember when I was a boy, thinking I would never be able even to get a note out of it, and then how it burst into life with a sound like a new born baby, setting my mother's ornaments trembling on the sideboard. And so was I, with excitement. About what? I didn't know then. The trepidation and exhilaration of performing was still to come.

Could you perhaps manage to come to the RPO's Swansea concert? It would make me very proud indeed. I'll get you (and Beryl) the best seats in the hall and we can all go to the Bay View hotel afterwards. Give my very best to everyone in the band. I'll soak up all the news when I see you.

Until the 23rd.

Terry Johns

LETTERS, LINES AND SPACES

WALTER MURFIN AND I PLAYED IN THE GLAMORGAN YOUTH ORCHESTRA TOGETHER. HE LATER QUALIFIED AS A DOCTOR AND WENT INTO GENERAL PRACTICE IN TYWYN MERIONETHSHIRE.

Dr Walter Murfin
Glaslyn
LLANDUDNO
Gwynedd

27 Watermill Close
Ham
Richmond

1st May 1966

Dear Wally

You are a doctor at last! What a feeling that must give you and no one has ever deserved it more: all that midnight oil and self-denial! You're phenomenal I'll bet you never play the horn now.

You were always so much better than I was. I had an idea that you understood the physical side much better than I did. The muscles in the face are so small. When I changed from the cornet to the horn the different mouthpiece felt like a massive prosthesis. I remember thinking that the blowing of brass instruments is an absurd human activity but I suppose, no more so than sex or pole vaulting. I don't think you ever felt the lust for the musical life did you? That was what overrode every other thing for me and I have, from time to time, quite strong feelings of guilt about what I do. I can't help feeling that some day I'll be brought to account for the fact that I've never done an honest day's work in my life, and as I write this I remember all those nights you spent over your medical books after practicing with the youth orchestra all day. Anything that involved real work never came very easily to me.

I was disappointed that you weren't able to get to the concert in Aberystwyth, but it was a lovely surprise to see your mother. When she told me that you were delivering a baby, she looked so proud and I formed a mental picture of you, in the hospital on the hill, with lots of hot water and everything that I couldn't get out of my mind all evening.

LETTERS, LINES AND SPACES

To bring a human being into the world, and on a Thursday night in Aberystwyth too! That's really is a proper job!! I'm sure that's what my mother wanted for me.

I think I told you once that her first child was stillborn and I'm certain that it affected her a great deal. Life for her was always what could have been you know, and father took a lot of psychological punishment for that. Their life together as I remember it was continual conflict. My father on the other hand, and despite having worked at Tower colliery since his fourteenth birthday, really loved life, and he and I never argued about anything, but I do remember him looking at me in a very strange way one evening when I complained about how "tiring" my job was. The expression on his face was enough. I was careful what I said on that subject after that.

Guests at receptions ask us very often what we do "for a living" or what our "real job" is. I have a really good friend in the orchestra, who, when faced with such questions, lets his imagination get the better of him and turns into an ostrich farmer or an archaeologist. He was once a priest whilst talking to a very young wife of a very old Lord someone or other. She ended the evening in complete confusion, having been converted to Catholicism and become infatuated with her priest all at the same time. Pat has considerable knowledge about a great many subjects. This is what fuels his imagination so perfectly. Sometimes I wish I had put my time at grammar school to better use but I'd no interest in anything but music and English, so I keep quiet at receptions and watch the wondrous Royal Philharmonic enchanting and amusing the Americans across the continent.

At the end of seven hours on the chartered flight from Philadelphia, and four hours in the buffet car on the train to Cardiff, I spent Christmas in Wales, and the great day dawned for me when I was dragged painfully to consciousness by the sound of the band playing "Christians Awake" under my bedroom window, reminding me that I'd promised to be at the band room at eight thirty. Mother hadn't enough crockery to give everybody tea, so sweet sherry and beer were passed around in the garden while I got myself dressed.

I emerged into the blinding winter sunshine to be handed a flugelhorn. I hadn't blown one for years but after three or four carols played standing on the snow at various street corners I began to get the hang of it again. We made our way to the top of the town to the Miners' Club for the midday carol concert with the male voice choir. Emrys Evans the steward brought in a tray of roast potatoes when we arrived and a few of these washed down with beer served as a welcome, if unconventional breakfast. There were some lovely solos given by the choir members and my uncle Reg sang "Mary's Boy Child" insisting that I play the piano for him, which was a relief, to the club pianist who told me that he found it impossible to cope with Reg's sudden changes of key? For myself, I must say that I had (as a young man and Reg's "official" accompanist) found them invaluable aids to the development of my keyboard harmony skills. Reg has a lovely tenor voice, so the harmonic exploration is well worth the effort.

I hope that you enjoyed your Christmas, as much as I did mine. I certainly enjoyed Aberystwyth in Spring when we stayed at the White Horse, the landlord of which, as you may know suffers with insomnia and is incurably sociable, so after we'd played darts in the bar until about 2.00am he brought us fried egg and bacon sandwiches in the hope, I suspect of selling some more beer. I went for a solitary walk on the beach at that point in order to clear my head.

What a fantastic moonlit night it was. I thought of you up there in the hospital with all that blood, water and screaming new life and of your mother as I had seen her earlier at the concert. I'd forgotten what a handsome woman she was, and she looks splendidly isolated now in her widowhood. She seems to be full of confidence and optimism as if she's really grateful for what she's had, and eager for what's to come.

I'm so sorry to have missed you. I don't know when the orchestra will be in Wales again, the future being quite uncertain, but I'm determined to adopt the attitude that the other, more experienced players have to all this Arts Council malevolence towards us. We performed Elgar's "The Music Makers" a few weeks ago with Adrian Boult and I read the poem by O'Shaughnessy that was printed in the programme. It describes a life spent making music as a sort of dream - a kind of isolation. Some unavoidable destiny that Elgar understands perfectly as a kind of melancholy.

> We are the music makers
> And we are the dreamers of dreams
> Wandering by lone sea-breakers
> And sitting by desolate streams -
> World losers and world-forsakers
> On whom the pale moon gleams:
> Yet we are the movers and shakers
> Of the world forever, it seems.

That's how it begins. Isn't it beautiful? I've kept it in my horn case, which now holds quite a few things to comfort the traveller. I'm off again soon, this time to Europe with the London Mozart Players. Rome, Amsterdam, Paris and Milan all new to me of course, so the excitement continues, and you and I won't meet for a while yet but I'll write when I can.

Kind regards – unlimited admiration to your mother, and a long and healthy life to your first delivered child.

Yours ever

Terry J

LETTERS, LINES AND SPACES

"Puffed up and pickled in American generosity"

GARFIELD GRIFFITHS WAS MY ENGLISH TEACHER AT ABERDARE GRAMMAR SCHOOL. HE INTRODUCED ME TO THE WRITINGS OF JOYCE AND HENRY JAMES, WHOSE WORKS WERE NOT USUALLY INCLUDED IN THE SYLLABUS FOR OUR EXAMINATIONS. HE ALSO INTRODUCED ME TO THE POETRY OF WALT WHITMAN AND WILFRED OWEN THAT HAD BEEN SET TO MUSIC BY DELIUS AND BENJAMIN BRITTEN.

Mr. Garfield Griffiths
34 Glannant Street
ABERDARE
Glamorgan

Roma
Italia

9th July 1966

Dear Mr. Griffiths

I'm writing at a very grand mahogany desk, with a wine-coloured leather top. In front of me, below the high window, lies an old Roman square with a fountain at its centre. The heat of the midday sun keeps most Romans in cool darkness behind shuttered

LETTERS, LINES AND SPACES

windows but I'll have to go out presently to attend a reception at the British Embassy, which is one of the events that are the least exciting moments in our life on tour. I would much prefer to stay in this sumptuous hotel room writing letters and sending occasionally for a cool drink but we are expected to attend, and be sociable.

The rehearsal this morning was short and started very early so as to avoid working during the hottest part of the day, so I have been sitting here for hours, it seems, with my letters and postcards. I don't know many people here and players in chamber orchestras are a lot more reserved than the ones I'm used to playing with. There aren't any brass players of course so the music is quieter as are the aeroplane cabins and receptions.

The music is a real joy. This evening we'll be playing the "London" symphony of Haydn and Mozart's "Haffner" symphony. Jacqueline Du Pré will perform the Haydn cello concerto. Someone said she is just 22 years old. She is very young certainly and beautiful too, but when she plays she treads a line between enthusiasm and aggression that some of the purists here find difficult to accept. I'm positive she will be very famous one day. The audiences love her certainly.

Since our last meeting I've toured the east coast of America with the Royal Philharmonic, which is now my permanent family. We were in Wales too, in the spring for six terrific concerts with Walter Susskind conducting. A very attractive young girl whom he presented as his niece was the centre of his attention throughout the entire trip. So much so that the longest rehearsal session was, I think forty minutes in the whole week. Chamber orchestras rehearsals are much more serious. The conductor of this one (The London Mozart Players) is Harry Blech who's "Blech Quartet " gave many of the National Gallery wartime concerts with Dame Myra Hess. He is a brilliant musician, deeply dedicated to Mozart and Haydn and very supportive to young players like Jacqueline. He invited me to play with the Mozart Players while I was still studying at the Academy. What an opportunity that was!

LETTERS, LINES AND SPACES

I had never worn tails before nor did I possess any. A viola player from Toronto – a reserved sophisticated man, whose room with its velvet curtains and bone china was a haven of comfort amidst the semi squalor of our student house, invited me in one evening. He taught me to tie a bow and let me borrow his suit until I was able to acquire one for myself, and I emerged the next day on to the stage of the City Hall in Leeds for my first professional engagement. As great an opportunity as it was I couldn't say that I enjoyed it greatly. I did spend almost the whole day without speaking to anyone and the conversations I overheard were invariably about dots, lines and the minutiae of music. To mention such things in the RPO would be like talking about sex to your grandmother.

On the return journey from Leeds, in the back of someone's car at midnight and, bored stiff on the edge of a discussion about Christine Keeler and National security I did seriously consider going back to Wales to play the piano in pubs or the cornet in brass bands. Because, at that time, never having played with the Royal Philharmonic, I had no idea how much joy and fun there could be in a musician's life.

Sitting here, and facing the prospect of exploring Rome alone after the concert, I miss the laughter, irreverence and cynicism of that orchestra. The uncertainty too, is something I've almost come to depend upon. It sets my blood racing and reminds me I'm alive. After the concert I shall go to see the Trevi fountain, which I'm told, is most beautiful after dark, tomorrow we'll be in Paris!! I must dress for the reception and get a hold on myself.

5.30pm
The reception was not nearly as boring as I expected it would be and the food was more delicious than anything I have ever tasted. Salmon in aspic, cold lobster with asparagus; these things are all new experiences for me. I spoke to a few people, none of whom were Romans or even Italians. An ultra polite American introduced himself to

me, saying that he was part of the Shell Company that sponsors hundreds of concerts throughout the world. Whilst he was speaking to me, I found myself distracted by the memory of an incident at a reception given for the RPO when a very grand lady announced to one of the trombone players that her husband was "in oil". The player in question took a deep breath against the effect of a great deal of Embassy champagne, and enquired if her husband was a "sardine"? I couldn't erase the incident from my mind while the Shell man was talking, so I made an excuse and retired to a quiet corner of the room to avoid embarrassing myself. Looking at the fabulous display of food and drink at the reception, I remembered Joyce and the Misses Morkan's annual dance in "Dubliners". His description of the buffet spread out on the table and the square piano in that old Dublin house has stayed with me for years.

I still love to read, which I attribute entirely to your influence and have hours on aeroplanes and trains to spend doing it. Do you remember lending me your copy of Henry James' "Washington Square"? I'm ashamed to tell you that I still have it. I re-read it recently in New York (for added effect) and having finished it, I sincerely intend to post it to you, with what will be a good deal of relief for us both I'm sure. Thank you for being so patient about it, and for the benefit of all the other books from your library that you loaned to me.

The connection between music and literature has become real to me now. When I took part in Britten's War Requiem last year, I knew Wilfred Owen's poems from our English classes in Aberdare so hearing the piece for the first time and live was a significant experience indeed. It struck me how the discussion among the performers was almost always about the music. The poetry was seldom mentioned except by Britten himself, who was conducting and spent a lot of time with the chorus, trying to get real clarity in the pronunciation, and meaning, of the text.

I find myself becoming much more grateful for my education as the benefits of it are now becoming obvious to me. I remember you and Gethin Evans both saying that education had to be a priority in society; that it was the key to real equality and fairness between people.

When I was at the Academy, my father who hadn't a telephone had occasion to write to me about an important matter. I had never seen his handwriting before except as his signature and for the first time I realised that writing and spelling were an enormous effort for him. His parents could neither read nor write and he was compelled by his father's early death to leave school at the age of fourteen in order to support the family. He never spoke about it to me; it was one of my mother's many sisters who told me the story shortly before I left for my first term at the Academy. I'm sure he felt ashamed and frustrated because he couldn't involve himself in my education. Reading his letter that day had a great effect on me, my earliest memories of him being his tireless working and perpetual semi-poverty. Education gives us privileged ones some control over our own lives.

Privilege, that's what I feel sitting here in this luxury and in the excitement of what's to come. Maybe one day I'll have a family of my own. How is your family? Are they looking forward to your retirement? You will have the time at last to re-read the books you always wanted to. I'm sure you will miss the old school. The old school will miss you most certainly and this little orchestra will miss me if I'm not on the platform at 7.30 so I must change my clothes. There are a few people walking in the square now and it feels much cooler.

Did you tell me that Joyce was attacked and robbed just before he left Rome? I'll be careful at the Trevi fountain, not to look like a tourist. Goodbye for now. Many thanks for everything. A long and happy retirement and all the salmon in the Usk.

Yours ever

Terry Johns

LETTERS, LINES AND SPACES

PS I will return the book. I promise you it has not been touched by beer or marmalade.

LETTERS, LINES AND SPACES

Tubby Hayes – Freddy Logan Afro-Cuban Big Band In The Marquee 1964

GETHIN EVANS WAS MUSIC MASTER AT ABERDARE. BOB JONES AND I FORMED HIS ENTIRE SIXTH FORM MUSIC CLASS, AND AFTER SCHOOL WE OFTEN PLAYED JAZZ TOGETHER, AND MADE WILD PLANS FOR OUR FUTURE. IN HIS LATER LIFE, BOB TAUGHT FRENCH AND PLAYED JAZZ PIANO.

1969 WAS THE YEAR OF ENOCH POWELL'S INFAMOUS "RIVERS OF BLOOD" SPEECH, AND IN THOSE TIMES, THERE WERE CLEAR BOUNDARIES BETWEEN "POP" AND "CLASSICAL MUSIC" THAT WERE CONSIDERED BY SOME, TO BE INVIOLABLE.

MANY PEOPLE, EVEN ESTABLISHMENT FIGURES IN MUSIC, THOUGHT IT INAPPROPRIATE THAT THE "ROYAL PHILHARMONIC SHOULD SHARE A STAGE WITH "DEEP PURPLE".

Mr. Robert Jones   27 Watermill Close
34 Park Terrace   Ham
ABERDARE   Richmond
Glamorgan

18th September 1969

LETTERS, LINES AND SPACES

Dear Bob

I'm writing to your Aberdare address as you can see. I was in Paris in the summer and an entirely impromptu visit to the address that I had for you there was unsuccessful. A shrugging Frenchman weighed down with groceries told me that if you were the person he thought I was enquiring after that you wouldn't be back in Paris until September. I could hear the sound of a piano coming from the top of the building but I was certain it wasn't you playing it because it wasn't very good and it wasn't jazz. I was really disappointed to have missed you, hoping that we could have visited a club or two. I can tell you that no one in the London Mozart Players has the slightest interest in jazz or would consider going out after midnight and although the music was terrific, at the end of the tour I found myself in various states of depression, delusion, psychosis and eventually despair. I was greatly relieved to get back to London.

I had no right to feel such hostility towards a whole group of people in this way. My feelings were simply a result of class difference I'm sure, so I told myself that the people from musical families and the "middle class" had no more influence on the circumstances of their birth than did I, and as soon as I got to London I headed for the West End to find somewhere to play. I'm almost always welcome with a French horn. Its sound adds something unique to a group and I seem to be the only person in London who wants to play jazz on it. Before I left for the tour I played with Tubby Hayes and Freddie Logan's Afro Cuban Big Band at the Marquee Club, and I'll be doing some BBC "Jazz in Britain" broadcasts with Kenny Wheeler and Graham Collier. If I thought I could make any kind of living playing jazz I'd do it like a flash. Jazz musicians are the very best of people and anything and everything in their lives is fuel for humour. I was in the Marquee club the other day, with Harry Becket, Joe Harriot, and a few white guys, all laughing and joking about Powell's "Rivers of Blood" speech. Bob there was no trace of anything in that room, but the ridiculous. No high horses, opinions or resentments. These guys just love one another. Music and life are synonymous to them and there seems to be almost no rivalry but a great deal of warmth and companionship.

LETTERS, LINES AND SPACES

I'm sure that you will be playing a lot in Paris; the jazz scene there is vigorous isn't it? I hope you will write and tell me all about it.

The Royal Philharmonic has a European tour next year. I'll come and see you (by arrangement this time) and we can maybe hit Paris with some of our old tunes. Henry Lowther taught me to phrase in long lines and to study the way Miles Davis did it. That style suits the horn perfectly. I'd love to try a few things with you. It'd be like the old days.

My conversation with your Parisian neighbour was the first time I had attempted to speak French since I left school. He understood me well enough I think, but it required a big effort on my part. I will try harder! You must dream in French by now do you not?

I imagine you in Montmartre in the small hours in amongst the cognoscenti talking about jazz and Engels. Do you still smoke those Gauloises? I smoke more heavily than ever now and have acquired a taste for American cigarettes.

When I was in the US, I went with a group of players from the Royal Philharmonic to see Sonny Rollins at the Half Note in New York and he played fabulously to a club that was packed to capacity. When I heard him at Ronnie Scott's there may have been a dozen people listening, but his performance was astonishing all the same. You will have your club one day, I'm certain of that and you can have him there and play yourself too. Why don't you do it in Cardiff? Would that be the first ever jazz club in the city? What a thing!!

We could really live the Bohemia and Saturnalia we dreamed of as boys.

You would enjoy the Royal Philharmonic. It's full of eccentric people from the most unlikely origins. There's a Canadian Ukrainian violinist who lives in a Volkswagen camper van when the orchestra is touring in Britain and dines alone every night on fish he catches where he can, or on fresh meat from local butchers, soaked in wine marinade. Tins of smoked oysters, asparagus, and local cheeses add the variety and occasionally he entertains one or two guests. I was among the privileged, one lovely spring night in Wales and spent the evening on a riverbank laughing at his tales of Tommy Beecham and the old days.

Another violinist, a Scotsman, arrived at Heathrow airport in full evening dress at eight o'clock in the morning for a three week tour of America. His apparel provoked not the slightest comment from the other men or the cocktail barman in the departure lounge who greeted him, as an old friend. Throughout the twenty thousand miles across the Atlantic and three or four American states, he travelled in the same clothes and carrying only a change of shirt, a toothbrush and consecutive bottles of whisky in his airline bag. There are so many other eccentrics too. I will get to know them better I'm sure, though most keep themselves to themselves.

I'll be back amongst them tomorrow. We have rehearsals for a concert with a group called Deep Purple. The concert will be at the Albert Hall and has already given rise to a fair amount of controversy. People are saying, for some reason that the Royal Philharmonic oughtn't to be performing with pop groups. It's all expected to be in the papers.

I might say that these complainants are some of the same people that advocate the cutting of state funding to the orchestra. I find all this acrimony to be very tiresome to say the least. Personally I'm looking forward to the concert hugely. Jon Lord has written a piece specially for the group and orchestra conducted by Malcolm Arnold and it will all be televised. Fuck the Arts Council!!!

Will you write to tell me all about the Paris jazz scene and what happened to that French "assistante" you were running around with in Cardiff? I'll be in London for a while now, recording mostly until we leave again for a German tour in November.

LETTERS, LINES AND SPACES

I received a letter from Gethin Evans a few days ago. He's well and politely enquiring about everyone in between choir training, piano teaching, chapel organing, conducting and everything else. He's a real gem. I hope I will hear from you soon.

Best Wishes

Terry Johns

PS   I played on the film "Custer of the West" which will be released next year. Films are great fun.

LETTERS, LINES AND SPACES

THE PERFORMANCE, AT THE ALBERT HALL OF JON LORD'S CONCERTO FOR GROUP AND ORCHESTRA, TOGETHER WITH THE FILM" 200 MOTELS", STARRING FRANK ZAPPA AND THE 'MOTHERS OF INVENTION', MADE POP MUSIC HISTORY AND HELPED TO KEEP THE ORCHESTRA FROM FINANCIAL RUIN.

MARTIN SHILLITO JOINED THE ROYAL PHILHARMONIC IN 1965, AND I JOINED THAT ORCHESTRA SHORTLY AFTERWARDS, BUT A FEW YEARS LATER THE LONDON SYMPHONY ORCHESTRA WERE MAKING STRENUOUS EFFORTS TO PERSUADE HIM TO JOIN THEM.

9 Edwardes Square
Knightsbridge
LONDON

The George Hotel
STAMFORD
Lincs

20th September 1969

Dear Martin

Wilton is a hell of a place. I don't think it's a place at all! At least we were unable to find it on any map. The concert, which you so cleverly avoided was sponsored by ICI and took place in a tent, which was the largest in a group of tents, pitched in the middle of a vast field. There were no proper buildings or lavatories to be found. And it rained heavily for the whole day so that when we tried to escape to find food between the rehearsal and the concert most of the cars had lodged themselves firmly in the mud.

Six of us jammed ourselves into Cecil James' Rover, which he had wisely parked on a solid patch of ground outside the gate and he drove us all up to Redcar, which because it was Sunday was entirely closed. The trombones, not to be defeated, hammered on the door of a shabby little Chinese restaurant, the proprietor of which let us in out of the rain, and was only too happy to serve the six of us with won ton soup and a very large and delicious Chow mein made with half a dozen varieties of shellfish and chicken. The three trombones drank his entire stock of Guinness and the rest of us had wine, so we had something to inure us to the performance to come, which was the Beethoven Missa

LETTERS, LINES AND SPACES

Solemnis conducted by Stamford Robinson and largely obscured by the sound of the rain on the canvas above. After the concert we drove down to the George at Stamford, which is where we are just now.

How did your concert go? The Times this morning said a lot about Bernstein and his "flamboyant style" but nothing much about the Mahler symphony or the performance. Obviously I'd be delighted for you if you were invited to join the LSO but it would make life difficult here without you. Why can't you stay here? Life is a good deal less hectic and I do think we have more fun by and large.

Anyway! I shouldn't try to influence you. It's just that I do think you're the best and I hope you don't think that I don't appreciate that. The LSO obviously do. I wish you well and I'll miss you if (when) you go. I somehow imagined that we two would play in an orchestra together but for longer. I wonder too at times how it is that we get on so well considering our wildly different backgrounds. When I spent the night at your house in Edwardes Square after that Prom I have to admit to feeling uncomfortable at breakfast with those linen napkins in silver rings and I couldn't help thinking about your staying at our house in Baptist Place without hot water or an insider lavatory.

I can see you now wandering down the garden path, in your Simpson's sports jacket carrying a bucket of water.

My mother altered her entire demeanour at the sound of a public school accent. She changed the way she spoke, the way she ate, even the way she sat or moved around. "Why did you bring him here" she growled at me while father patiently laid and lit the fire so we could have some breakfast. "He likes it here" I said. And a little later when the fire was glowing and the eggs were clucking in the frying pan I really felt that you did. You certainly had a smile on your face. I hope you don't think that my parents didn't like you. Mother's resentment was directed entirely at me I can assure you of that. She is a very difficult person to understand, and my father never speaks to anyone until he's known him or her for at least a year.

You missed a really great concert with Deep Purple the audience reaction was astonishing; far different from anything we're used to. I'm told that despite disapproval and criticism there will be more "pop" music on the schedule. The orchestra will be in a film with someone called Frank Zappa, who's been described as a genius by some and a charlatan by others?

Incidentally, on Wednesday last the first rehearsal of the Barry Tuckwell horn quartet took place at the house in Hamilton Terrace of Lord Harewood who is now Barry's brother-in-law. It's a very grand house indeed (complete with butler). I'm pretty sure from what Barry was inferring that you will be joining the LSO soon. Playing with him all the time will be a great thing for you. He is, I'm sure the best player in the world now. I heard recently his recording with Britten, Peter Pears and the LSO of the "Serenade" for tenor, horn and strings. Technically at least it's better than the Dennis Brain version. He makes the "Queen and Huntress" movement sound easy. Playing in the quartet with him however is far from easy, mainly because he makes such great demands on himself the whole time. One feels obligated to do the same. But he's a great man, a "human" person, and great fun. You'll have a great time in Florida too. Sid Weissbloom tells me that you'll be back on the 19th. There are rehearsals that day for Bruckner 7 with Erich Leinsdorf. Have you played for him? It'll be at the Festival hall, with proper lavatories and carpets instead of duckboards. And the old team will be together again.

Good Luck

Drac

LETTERS, LINES AND SPACES

CECIL JAMES WAS ONE OF THE MOST EMINENT WOODWIND PLAYERS IN BRITISH ORCHESTRAL HISTORY. HE WAS THE PRINCIPAL BASSOONIST OF THE ROYAL PHILHARMONIC ORCHESTRA AND A MEMBER OF THE DENNIS BRAIN WIND QUINTET.

Mr Barry Tuckwell   The George Hotel
London Symphony Orchestra   STAMFORD
                                                                           Lincs

11th April 1969

Dear Barry

We're at the George hotel in Stamford, on the Great North road, and very warm, and grand and ancient it is too!   A stark contrast to the muddy squalor of yesterday. We got here very late last night after a fucking awful day and a terrible performance of "Missa Solemnis" in a tent on a field. This morning I rushed downstairs to the dining room to try to salvage something from breakfast, only to find that the sideboard had been cleared of everything except a nearly empty coffee pot.

Cecil James was sitting, like George Sanders, in a great black leather chair, reading the Times and smoking a cigarette in an amber holder.

"Just like the trenches wasn't it ", he said, without looking up from his newspaper. "Uncle Wilfred was in the trenches you know. He remembered that the three worst things were the 'mud', the 'noise', and the 'frightful people you meet!'"

Cecil is not fond of "Missa Solemnis". He calls Beethoven the great "deaf" composer!

"Had he only realized that everyone could hear him perfectly well", Cecil says," the poor fellow would not have found it necessary to repeat himself so often!

LETTERS, LINES AND SPACES

I recently saw a copy of your LSO schedule for next year that includes two weeks in Florida amidst hundreds of recording sessions. I wouldn't expect anyone to resist such seduction, so despite having written a few straw clutching and valedictory lines to him, earlier this morning, I shan't blame Martin in the least when he leaves us. The beleaguered RPO can't provide its players with that kind of work, and I shall miss him, but I enjoy the RPO, and I belong here I believe.
I have come to thrive on insecurity and the fear of financial Armageddon that reminds me I'm alive during the endless rehearsals!

Despite the atrocious financial position, and the concerted mendacity of the critics, there is the stark reality that we have no choice but to pay extortionate fees to these "prestigious" conductors within thirty days, if we are to get any audience at all, while we ourselves haven't been paid for three months.

But the humour persists, to the eternal annoyance of our adversaries, things are improving gradually, and the enemy seems to be in retreat, or maybe just regrouping.

Memories of my first concerts with the LSO invoke fear and insecurity of a different kind.

During that "Rite of Spring" we played with Rodzhesvensky on fifteen minutes rehearsal, I felt the full terror of human sacrifice that Stravinsky was trying to convey, and there were a few frightened faces among the younger players, but Rodzhesvensky was absolutely relaxed and faultlessly clear, and the performance was tremendous!

You will remember another concert in that series that included huge wedges of Gotterdammerung with Birgit Nielsen and Stokowski, who managed to get himself completely lost for about five minutes as I recall. The LSO completely ignored him of course and even managed a creditable performance. The reviews in the next day's

LETTERS, LINES AND SPACES

newspapers covered the "Maestro" in glory but the interesting thing for me is that I don't think the RPO could have taken charge collectively in that way.

I was scared stiff at my first concert with the LSO and I'm sure you knew that. People were great to me – no reassurances or anything. I felt just like a professional player engaged for the day. They are a great bunch.

There are a lot of fascinating, colourful people in the Royal Phil. too, and nicknames abound.

"The Wooden Indian", with his great Roman nose, and over- dyed black hair, sitting behind his grumbling double bass, has hardly uttered a word for twenty years they say.

"The Count of no account" in a hotel lobby, will offer you a Turkish cigarette from his solid silver, monogrammed case, whilst waiting for a member of staff to respond to his complaints about the temperature or situation of his room. Then there is the cadaverous, chain smoking, veteran bassoonist, who played for Elgar and Strauss. He's known as "The Stick Insect". There are some others too, like "The Undertaker", and "The non- magnetic Pole". You'll recognize them instantly!

Roger Briggs played for Elgar and Henry Wood, and has been a cellist here since Beecham. You'll remember him by his ancient trilby, and his false teeth that slip down when he laughs.

As much as he loves the company of the younger players, he has given up trying to remember all their names so he simply calls everyone Tony! This device works comfortably for him and all his young friends, because he does it with such old English charm and fatherly affection that no one minds in the least. He won't tour now because he's tired of hotels and airports so a group of us, on a charter flight to New York celebrated his seventieth birthday, in his absence, with some BEA champagne. The stewardesses were a little bewildered while serving us, (all calling each other Tony!). Touring with this orchestra provides some lovely moments I can tell you.

I'll see you on the 12th and later in the year for Mahler and Horenstein.

You can tell me all about him when I see you.

Yours ever

Drac

P.S.   You'll have to tell me all about André Previn too. I know he's a terrific jazz pianist.   I still have his "My Fair Lady" LP.

LETTERS, LINES AND SPACES

The Philadelphia Four (l-r Evan Watkin, John Davies, Me, Harry Jones)

ON THE 18TH OF JUNE 1970 NEIL KINNOCK WAS ELECTED AS LABOUR MEMBER OF PARLIAMENT FOR BEDWELLTY. HE BECAME LEADER OF THE BRITISH LABOUR PARTY IN 1983. AS A YOUNG MAN HE SANG IN THE GLAMORGAN YOUTH CHOIR AND I PLAYED IN THE ORCHESTRA THAT ACCOMPANIED THEIR CONCERTS.

NEIL DID A GREAT DEAL BEHIND THE SCENES TO HELP THE MUSICIANS' STRUGGLE AGAINST THE BBC IN 1980.

Mr. Neil Kinnock   George Hotel
11 Ash Court   STAMFORD
BLACKWOOD   Lincs
Gwent

                                                                April 1969

Dear Neil

LETTERS, LINES AND SPACES

I'm here in Stamford, with some time to write some letters. I also was able to read the Times this morning, and it occurred to me going through a piece about Harold Wilson that you will most probably be a Labour member of parliament very soon and in a Labour government too! These are exciting times I feel in Britain and especially in music. London is the acknowledged musical capital of the world now, and every top conductor wants to work with a London orchestra. This government does at least provide some support for music and the arts and the music profession will be eternally grateful to Wilson and Lord Goodman for stopping the butchery of the BBC orchestras.

I've been a member of the Royal Philharmonic now for four years and the orchestra has really been through some hard times with the Arts Council. There's strong opposition to its very existence in some quarters. Anyway we're still around. You and Glenys must come to a concert in London when you are able to find the time. You will enjoy living here, I'm sure. Will you invite me to Westminster when you are elected?

I feel at home in London now. I've been here since 1962 when I arrived as a music student at the Royal Academy. Those were great days, when Christine Keeler, Alistair Sim and Trevor Howard used to come in to the Academy pub, and I had a job playing in the pit orchestra for "Oliver" at the New Theatre. It meant that I spent a lot of time around Soho, which was full of fascinating places and people. I played a lot of jazz at that time and the scene was very exciting, with Tubby Hayes and Stan Tracey playing at Ronnie Scott's nearly every night in between visiting Americans.

The "French" pub in Dean Street was packed daily with foreign sailors, artists, journalists and professional ladies, many of them French who would come in for a glass of Pernod but if anyone approached them they would shout for help to Gaston Berlemont the charming Belgian landlord who seemed to be equally comfortable talking to Francis Bacon as to a large cantankerous drunk. The place was classless and the atmosphere bizarre. Poets, artists and the criminal classes were all equally at home there. I loved it – the contraption screwed to the bar that dripped water through a lump of sugar on a leaf shaped spoon over a glass of absinthe – and of course there was always someone to drink with.

I still go there when I can.

The New Theatre was almost always full, it was an extraordinary thing. That show was so successful and the American tourists came in their thousands in the summer. Music must be a massive boost to the economy isn't it? I never hear anyone say so. Certainly no politician I've heard has ever said it. The film of "Oliver" has been a huge hit too, and made millions I suspect. I was fortunate enough to have played on a few of the sound track sessions. The great Johnny Green (Body and Soul) was conducting for a lot of the time and the orchestra was fantastic – made up mostly from London session players. Many men I know who play in symphony orchestras all the time would dearly love to spend their lives in studios, but for myself I like touring and concerts too much to give them up even for all that money.

I like chamber music too and I'm rehearsing right now for the Aldeburgh festival and a concert with the Tuckwell Horn Quartet. Session players don't get to do that kind of performing as a rule.

I'm sure you'll be elected as member for Bedwellty. Does the Conservative poll any votes there at all?   Is there a Tory brave enough to stand? You'll be another Bevan. Leader of the party. Prime Minister even!

One thing I find difficult to accept about that which I still consider to be my "new" life in England is the fact that many musicians are Tories, and like you as a Welshman, being surrounded by Conservative opinion doesn't feel comfortable to me at all. When one considers that every player in a London orchestra, or a BBC one is almost entirely dependent on public money for his livelihood it's puzzling to say the least. Hardly anyone takes any interest in the activities of the union, though it is very strong and the

LETTERS, LINES AND SPACES

fees are good. I read a bit about the beginnings of the Musicians' Union and the older men in the RPO have told me lots of stories about the old music hall and cinema orchestras when you often had to fight for your money at the end of the week.

The RPO string players are a rich mixture of European Jews that came to Britain to escape Hitler in the thirties, Irish and Scottish fiddlers with folk connections and a few "academics" for good measure. The brass and wind players are a blend of people like Cecil James and Leonard Brain who descend from musical "dynasties", and most of the rest came up through military and brass bands. Many learned their trade in tearooms, ships' orchestras, theatre pits and circuses so the self-preservation instinct is a very strong one here, not surprisingly I suppose.

There are, including myself, four Welshmen in the orchestra. We were entertained recently, in Philadelphia by a Welsh society of lawyers. They gave us a fantastic seafood dinner and we played a little something for them afterwards. We couldn't find anything published for violin, viola, trombone and horn so it fell to me to write something. I found a lovely old Welsh folk melody and arranged if accordingly. It felt good writing again. I hadn't done it for a while.

During the evening one of our hosts showed me a copy of the "Penguin Dictionary of Surnames" which states that the explorer John Cabot gave America its name, wishing to honour the chief investor in his voyage, the Welshman, Richard Ameryk (originally spelled Ap Meryke). The more familiar claims of Amerigo Vespucci were dismissed as "frivolous" by the dictionary's author.

The Welsh do "huddle" a lot don't they? I found myself in the "Gluepot" the other day with the 'Philadelphia Quartet', as we are now known, plus Geraint Evans who was singing on some opera recordings with the orchestra. He always makes straight for us whenever he's singing with the RPO. I'm sure Welsh MPs will behave similarly.

LETTERS, LINES AND SPACES

Have you seen "Battle of Britain"?   If you have, you'll have heard it with the music of Ron Goodwin, almost all the original music of William Walton having been replaced at the last minute by Harry Saltzman (I tell you this remembering your excitement on hearing Belshazzar's Feast for the first time when we were on that Glamorgan Youth Choir course together). Olivier, when he heard of the studio's decision, threatened to remove his name from the credits. So to appease him Walton's music for the "Battle in the Air" remains in the film and transforms it from that point, I think. There has been a hell of a lot of disquiet in high places about the studio's decision I'm told, including a rumour that Ted Heath, being a musician and a friend of Walton, is most annoyed by it.

Many people are ignorant and unkind about Heath's musicianship you know. He was an organ scholar at Oxford. I've played for him a couple of times and I can tell you, there are a lot worse that call themselves "professionals".

Anyway when you've seen the film (which is otherwise terrific!) I'll be interested to hear your comments. I forgot to say that I played on the Walton sessions for the film and was then "sacked" from the sound stage at Denham along with Malcolm Arnold and a fair sized orchestra, only hope that Walton's music is preserved if only as a concert piece. It is, as you would expect, superbly written. I don't want to be in years to come, one of the few people ever to have heard it.

I'll be leaving, in a day or two for Prague and the spring festival. This is a date in the RPO diary, which was cancelled when the Russians invaded but has now been reinstated for the sake of diplomacy, we are told. We will have to play a lot of Dvorak (including the New World Symphony with Rudolph Kempe), which is a tall order for any orchestra. We received also, from the tour agent a printed guide telling us how to behave and what to do and say should we be arrested, so I'm hoping to avoid upsetting

LETTERS, LINES AND SPACES

the Russians and to be back in Blighty for the Aldeburgh festival and the Edinburgh festival too.

Something tells me it's time to start for London so let me wish you success in the election when it comes. I know you will continue the fight until we get something decent for ordinary people in Britain. My apologies for being generous and fair minded about Ted Heath. I don't know what came over me, I promise not to do it in the Miners' Club or in front of father.

Yours ever

Drac

PS   When you are installed at Westminster, we'll have a day out in London. I'll take you to the "French pub". I'd love you to bring Glenys so long as she's prepared to drink with whores and gangsters and to let Gaston Berlemont "groom" his great moustache on her hand.

LETTERS, LINES AND SPACES

SOVIET TROOPS INVADED CZECHOSLOVAKIA IN AUGUST 1968. THE APPEARANCE OF THE ROYAL PHILHARMONIC AT THE PRAGUE SPRING FESTIVAL IN THE FOLLOWING YEAR WENT AHEAD AS PLANNED, BUT ONLY AFTER A GREAT DEAL OF DIPLOMATIC NEGOTIATION.

Mr Robert Jones
14 Rue de la Gare
PARIS 4

Ham
Richmond

25th May 1969

Dear Bob

What a surprise it was to hear from you again! Thank you for all the news. You are having a great time in Paris aren't you? I often wish I were a jazz player. Your letter was on the mat when I got back to London after our trip to Prague, which was nothing like we expected. I didn't see any Russians (in uniform anyway).

I remember Dexter Gordon appearing at Ronnie Scott's when I was a student. He didn't play much at all as I recall. He was a little "out of sorts" I think. What he did play I remember very well. He was a sensational player and from what you said in your letter, he still is. You saw Phil Woods too! Do you ever get the chance to play with any of these people?

I'll be in Edinburgh for the first week of the festival in August, so we can meet for certain. I'll look forward to it immensely.

Our visit to Prague was eventful to say the least. Certainly a lot of things happened which wouldn't have happened in England. The Czech Philharmonic put on a most lavish reception for us before our big Dvorak concert on the last night of the festival. A round little man called Czerny, who was one of the horn players there and a sort of human "beer barrel" decided that he was my "brother" which seemed to be one of the few English words he knew. So for the rest of the day and into the early hours of the next morning he took complete charge of my diet, social calendar and itinerary. He sat through the concert which was, it has to be said, a miraculous display of professionalism by the orchestra, given the amount of Czech beer that had been consumed through the afternoon, and afterwards he latched himself firmly on to me again, whisking me off across the deserted city (officially the Russians had a curfew in force) in his car to a jazz club in a very dark basement.

When we went down, from the empty street into the tiny basement, which was packed with people, John (Jumbo) Wilbraham the RPO first trumpet and Harry Spain the bass trombone player, whose combined weight is around forty six stones, were already there and occupying most of the area in front of the tiny bandstand, with the trumpeter from the group on stage, who was already somewhat the worse for wear from welcoming these famous British brass players with Czech "champagne".

Seeing the condition of our host and his trumpet lying on the table among the wine bottles, Harry Spain, always stimulated by a little mischief, grinningly encouraged me to play "one number". To cut all this short I took over the trumpeting for the night while Czerny sat by the bandstand proposing the occasional toast to Bix Beiderbecke in between those to Dubcek, Janacek, Dvorak and Harold Wilson. We did manage a pretty good version of "Tenderly" as we entered the melancholy stage of the proceedings, by which time there was no drummer, who had disappeared at around 2.00am following a shouting contest and a light exchange of blows with a visiting "lady" friend.

The gaps in the story were filled in for me a week or so later by a chuckling Harry Spain who said that at least I had not made a complete fool of myself with the trumpet (I thought you might like to know that) despite innumerable bottles of Czech lager being sent up to the bandstand, bought by people who had been at the concert, and Jumbo and Harry trying to dispose of the thousands of black market Czech Krona they had accumulated.

LETTERS, LINES AND SPACES

We arrived back at the orchestra hotel in time for a quick breakfast of salmon caviar, boiled eggs and white wine before taking the bus to the airport.

When I left Czerny at the departure gate he looked as if he had just returned from a health farm. I passed out in my seat on the plane and having slept the entire journey through, arrived at Heathrow in the most deplorable condition. My "fat" lip made me think I'd been fighting, and then I remembered the trumpet. It was great fun actually and a good time was had by all! My lip had recovered its composure by the evening of the following day, in time for my first Andre Previn session with the LSO. He is now the Principal Conductor of the Orchestra and I've certainly never seen anyone look less like a "Grand Maestro". In the breaks he wanders around talking to everyone, with none of that tortured genius bullshit. He loves people as much as he loves music it seems to me. We played the second symphony of Rachmaninoff straight through without much comment being made, but what he did say seemed to come from the composer in him that was the interesting thing. He seemed just to take delight in the LSO's playing while they played as if basking in sunlight and the luxury of not being interrupted. I'm sure I'll get to speak to him sometime soon. I'm itching to talk to him about Chet Baker, Sam Goldwyn and a thousand other people. Do you remember the "My Fair Lady" LP? How could you forget it? I think we nearly wore it out. That was really great jazz piano playing wasn't it? I wonder if people, when they listen to him play Rachmaninoff and Mozart, watch him conduct Vaughan Williams or his own music can begin to understand how much talent this man has. What complicates the image for conductor watchers of course is he being an approachable, reasonable and sociable human being. I'm certain that's the jazz player in him.

Let me know when you'll be in Edinburgh and where you'll be staying. We'll have a great time. There will certainly be somewhere we can play (but don't let me play the trumpet). Before we meet I'll be going to the Aldeburgh Festival for a little chamber

LETTERS, LINES AND SPACES

music concert, just with four French horns, which may not sound like much to you but is uniquely difficult and nerve wracking.

I was in Aberdare in the spring before Prague while the RPO was on a tour of Wales and I met your father in the "Boot" hotel. He looked hale and hearty and didn't appear to be ashamed or disappointed in the least about you or me being itinerant jongleurs and not having "proper" jobs. He seemed quite please about it. He's a great guy!

See you in August

Terry

LETTERS, LINES AND SPACES

THE MANCHESTER PULLMAN WAS A MAIN LINE LUXURY TRAIN WITH FIRST CLASS COACHES AND A STEWARD SERVICE. IT WAS WITHDRAWN FROM SERVICE IN 1985.

ONLY HOURS BEFORE THE 1969 ALDEBURGH FESTIVAL WAS DUE TO BEGIN, THE OLD BREWERY 'MALTINGS' AT SNAPE CAUGHT FIRE AND THE BUILDING WAS ALMOST COMPLETELY DESTROYED, BUT THE SCHEDULED CONCERTS WERE RE-LOCATED AND WENT AHEAD AS PLANNED. THE MORNING BROADCAST CONCERT WAS MY FIRST APPEARANCE WITH THE "BARRY TUCKWELL QUARTET".
MY OLD FRIEND BEN THOMAS WAS A VIOLA PLAYER FROM MORRISTON IN WALES. BEN DIED IN LONDON IN 1978.

Manchester Pullman

September 1969

Dear Ben

This train is full of muttering businessmen going north. It's an odd feeling to be travelling with the general public and all this grumbling reluctance!! I was captured by fog with the RPO at Dublin airport yesterday for five hours. The brass just had a party in the bar!!

You'll be wondering what happened to me at Aldeburgh! I arrived at the 'Plough & Sail' about a half hour after you'd left and spent some time talking to some English Chamber Orchestra Players, mainly about the fire of course, which by then had been all over the news. It had, they said, almost completely destroyed the Maltings, Ben Britten's piano and a great deal of music.

The Tuckwell horn quartet was forced to give its morning broadcast recital from the old church at Snape, which despite it being mid summer, was as cold as the grave.

LETTERS, LINES AND SPACES

My trembling, which I managed to bring under control in time for the broadcast, was a combination of anxiety, excitement and hypothermia, the journey from London to Snape in Barry's car having done nothing to help my condition. This was my first experience of his driving, and after a few terrifying encounters with tractors and farm animals, I felt sure it would be my last!

When we arrived finally at the church with fifteen minutes to spare before our 'live' broadcast at eleven o'clock, the beleaguered BBC producer who had been working since dawn to set up the equipment for the broadcast, (the fire having destroyed everything at the Maltings), was desperate for a few minutes to check the sound of the horns, so we did what we could and Barry played a few bars of the Beethoven Sonata with the piano.

The end of the concert was an immense relief to all of us, and we were driven to Ben Britten's house for a reception, where Peter Pears greeted us at the door, along with a very likeable lady, whom I later discovered to have been Imogen Holst, was serving sherry and canapés to everyone. She seemed to be fascinated, which was a surprise to me, by my valleys accent, and I think the sight of me swallowing those absurd canapés three at a time, alarmed her somewhat. So she took me to the kitchen and gave me a proper sandwich with a good slice of strong, salty cheese and a bottle of Guinness to wash it down.

Barry's promise of "breakfast on the way" had of course never materialized, so even before the concert started, I had been delirious with hunger.

Fortified by my sandwich and beer, I managed to mingle a bit and spoke to Britten for a while. He seemed fatalistic about the fire, hardly mentioning it at all. He was far more interested in the broadcast, saying how much he'd enjoyed the Tippet, and the sound of the horns in the church. Barry had insisted on a lot of rehearsal, and his own playing of course, is inspirational to everyone, so it was all a great success finally. Although as we left, I spotted the BBC producer sitting alone in the corner next to a table covered with empty plates and chicken bones, looking as if he'd seen the gates of hell!

When I got to the Plough & Sail, the landlord gave me your note saying you would be at Television Centre on the 25th. I'll be there too! I'm told it's going to be large orchestra for an hour-long show with Jack Jones, who's a really great singer so I'm looking forward to that. This is all to be conducted by Harry Betts who's very able and sociable, having been a trombone player in the Stan Kenton band. So we can all go to the Irish pub at Shepherd's Bush green, for boiled bacon and cabbage and Guinness.

The train is on the move now. Breakfast is served and the rain has started. I have a few pals in the Hallé to steer me around Manchester after the concert

Good luck

Drac

P.S. No one ever asked me to play with the English Chamber Orchestra. You must tell me all about it when we meet. The strings always sound superb to me on the broadcasts I've heard, and I imagine it must be marvellous to play in those Britten premiers.

LETTERS, LINES AND SPACES

In November 1970 I met Karin Bruce at the London Palladium.

Mr. Martin Shillito
London Symphony Orchestra

The Garden
Crooked Billet
Wimbledon

Dear Martin

Sunday morning on the common at Wimbledon! Lovely! - Frost is melting under the winter sun. Everything is shining and the weekend is winding down perfectly.

I went to Trattoria Terrazza last night, as nervous and excited as could be, to have dinner with an amazingly beautiful girl called Karin Bruce who, by divine providence and Royal command I met at the Palladium a few weeks ago.

I was playing in the stage orchestra for Andy Williams at the end of what turned out to be a very long show, and she was dancing in the chorus right at the beginning, but I did manage to find her during rehearsals among crowds of celebrities, jugglers, people with ladders, and a forest of ostrich feathers backstage and to speak to her for long enough to come away with her telephone number.

She is tall, dark and distractingly elegant, and her company is fascinating. In fact there seems to be hardly anything ordinary about her at all. She danced at the famous Casino in Beirut before the war, when it was the top nightspot in the world and Omar Sharif used to go there to play the tables.

We ate a seafood salad, "Sinatra" and the Terrazza's famous steak tartare, while she told me about the fabulous floorshow, with lions, elephants, Lebanese muscle men, acrobats and beautiful showgirls, all choreographed by Jack Coles who is famous in show business for having taught Marilyn Monroe to dance.

LETTERS, LINES AND SPACES

What a marvellous evening we had until she had to leave to go to a late night revue at L'Hirondelle, at which point I walked around the corner to the French pub to get an Armanac before heading home.

The eleven o'clock, last orders bell was ringing as I arrived, and you have to wade through a lot of human wreckage at that time on Saturday night to get a drink in the "French" but it's worth it because you almost always run in to someone you know.

Francesca Gabbara, the cellist was there last night with Ben Thomas, croaking and spluttering from "Senior Service" and gulping gin, en route for "Talk of the town". Their day had started at eight a.m. at Olympic studios in Barnes with some jingles for "Hotpoint washing machines, and toothpaste, followed by six hours at A.T.V. Elstree with Jack Parnell and a session somewhere else for George Martin. Shirley Bassey's late night cabaret seemed to form some sort of afterthought, like something for them to do on the way home, so somehow I didn't think they would be in the least interested by my dinner or my fabulous companion.

Having excused myself duties from the Royal Phil. for the weekend, it's a luxury not to have to go to the Albert hall for the Sunday Tchaikovsky extravaganza so I'm sitting here in the frosty garden of the Crooked Billet, waiting for beer, with a shemozzle of dogs around my feet who, knowing that it is exactly twelve o'clock and that there are always logs ablaze on the hearth in this pub, are fervently barking for the doors to open. I'm sorry to be so self indulgent and for not enquiring, until now, about your family, the L.S.O. Florida trip, new and inconspicuous motor car, physical and spiritual wellbeing and so on, but I really am, as you will no doubt have noticed, very taken with the lovely Karin Bruce.

I gather that until now, the men in her life have been acrobats, diplomats, and lion tamers so I'm wondering what she could find exciting about yours truly.

LETTERS, LINES AND SPACES

Good Luck and the best to Barry

Drac

LETTERS, LINES AND SPACES

In 1972 Martin Shillito acquired a Lotus sports car, which was wrecked on the Ipswich road, in a serious accident that he was fortunate to have survived.

Lorin Maazel's broadcast performance of Mahler's "Resurrection" symphony at the Royal Festival hall, fell sadly short of its spiritual aspirations, ending instead in an unpleasant backstage exchange of insults and accusations.

8 Ash Close

New Malden

Surrey

Dear Martin

What a shock I got when I heard you were in hospital, and discovered that you own a Lotus sports car or at least the fragmented remains of one. This leads me to suspect that the LSO pays you more money than you need, though not enough obviously, to allow you to buy postage stamps or spare coins for telephones.

Tuckwell tells me that thankfully, you are in one piece, and so a plan is forming to come and see you. You may of course need some time to explain why you were going to Ipswich and why you were in such a hurry to get there.

You must have heard by now about Maazel's BBC Mahler disaster. Contrary to anything you may have heard, the BBC stage management was almost entirely responsible for it. Having cleared the music stands, music and chairs from the off-stage area, after the morning rehearsal they omitted to put them back again for the concert in the evening.

LETTERS, LINES AND SPACES

I did actually get there in time, against the advice of the BBC person that was appointed to oversee the proceedings (He said I was panicking unnecessarily. He obviously wasn't, or he might have noticed that there was no music, chairs or anything else at the place where they ought to have been), but in the absence of any other stage band members I could only peer through an opening between the doors, watching Maazel as the great self-delusion hit him smack in the face with the Maestro's worst nightmare – SILENCE!! He made several self-important and pompous gestures to no avail. I think someone on the stage played something eventually, by this time I was distracted with planning my new career as a postman, having been told at age fourteen by my father's brother that mining would kill me in a fortnight.

Pat O'Brian maintains that conducting is not so much a vocation or a profession as a manifestation of a mental illness. Certainly, some of these people are not normal. Childish petulance arrogance and self-centeredness seems to be stock in trade for Maazel. His behaviour after the performance was definitely bordering on insanity, striding around the room, stripped to the waist, shouting and ranting at everybody. A great deal of it was directed at me for some reason that I can't account for.

The 'legendary' Neville Cardus didn't comment much on it. There was something in the review in the Guardian about Mazel having 'mistimed' the off-stage horn call. These are arguably the most important bars in the piece and the Guardian critic doesn't notice that nobody played. I suspect he was listening on the radio while doing something else. I accused him of that in a letter, which I don't expect to be published.

Barry says you are cheerful, and are expected to recover quickly and completely. I'm glad of that. It means that you could perhaps reply to any one of my three recent letters, now that you have time on your hands and the use of your arms. Tell me how much you are enjoying the LSO. Do you miss your itinerant RPO pals?

LETTERS, LINES AND SPACES

We're recording at Walthamstow next week. Cecil James and I will come up to see you. I'll telephone the hospital to make sure you are still alive etc. Don't want to drive all that way for nothing!!

Luv

Drac

P.S.   Do you know if they have a band in the Foreign Legion?

LETTERS, LINES AND SPACES

LORIN MAAZEL IS THE FRENCH BORN AMERICAN CONDUCTOR WHO WAS MUSIC DIRECTOR AT THE CLEVELAND ORCHESTRA, THE VIENNA STATE OPERA AND THE PHILHARMONIA OF LONDON.

Lorin Maazel   8 Ash Close
C/o BBC Symphony Orchestra   New Malden
Maida Vale Studios   Surrey
LONDON W9

Dear Lorin Maazel

This letter, written with some reluctance on my part, concerns the recent performance of Mahler's "Resurrection" symphony in which you directed the BBC Symphony Orchestra at the Royal Festival Hall.

I will begin by identifying myself. You will no doubt remember me as the horn player to whom you appeared to apportion the entire blame for the unfortunate absence of the off-stage players from their positions.

The torrential and ferocious verbal assault I was forced to endure would obviously have been spared to me had I been able to summon enough professionalism to play the parts of several other people (including my own) entirely from memory and from behind the stage. My only misdemeanour, it seems, was to be the only player to be where he ought to have been, and at the time appointed.

In the absence of music stands, music, several other players and the person, appointed to hold the door at the precise aperture according to your instructions, I decided that, discretion being the better part of valour, not to play at all would be the wisest course of action.

LETTERS, LINES AND SPACES

The absence of the necessary equipment from the 'crime' scene would seem to me to have been the clear responsibility of the BBC although there was no mention of this undeniable fact in your tirade against me.

Would it be churlish of me to suggest that your perfect and omnipotent self might have checked these important arrangements beforehand?

The dictatorial (almost wholly tolerated) and unreasonable blaming of others for one's shortcomings is a powerful weapon in the armoury of non-executive musicians such as yourself, reinforcing as it does to "maestrophiles", the illusion of power and indispensability that you have created for your miserable selves.

Had this outburst been an isolated incident of such hideous behaviour on your part, I would hope to have borne it with resolve and understanding. However, your demeanour seems to me to be a seamless sequence of petulance, vindictiveness, selfishness and meanness of spirit, the worst of all being bad manners which you seem to reserve purely for use against orchestral players, the very people that give you prominence and adulation in public, and glory in the eyes of the critics.

I should be grateful to God that no offensive weapons or firearms were close to hand at the Festival Hall the other night, for judging from the loss of control you had obviously suffered I would have been fortunate to have escaped with my life!
One more benefit derived for me from this debacle is of course, that I shall not be required to make further contact with you.

Gratefully

Terry Johns

LETTERS, LINES AND SPACES

NEVILLE CARDUS WAS THE CHIEF MUSIC CRITIC OF THE "GUARDIAN" NEWSPAPER.

Mr. Neville Cardus   8 Ash Close
'The Guardian'   New Malden
                                                                Surrey

                                                                1972

Dear Neville Cardus

Your recent review in the 'Guardian' newspaper, of Lorin Maazel's performance of Mahler's "Resurrection" symphony had special interest for me. I took part in the performance and was amazed at some of your observations.

Your statement that Mr Mazel had "mistimed" the off-stage horn call intrigued me. I was one of the off-stage players and I can tell you that despite three grandiloquent gestures from the podium it never sounded at all, at least not from behind the stage or with the sound of four horns according to Mahler's instructions. ---

One of the orchestral players **eventually** began to play from a fragment of a cue that was in his part ---

May I suggest that you were not present in the hall for the performance but listening to the BBC live broadcast? Furthermore I would suggest that had you the sureness of ear and knowledge of this great symphony, that this very act of journalistic criticism presupposes you to have, you would have perceived there to have been only one player playing the passage in question. And, most importantly, had you been actually present in the hall where the concert took place, that the player was not playing "off stage", according to Mahler's instructions.

LETTERS, LINES AND SPACES

Perhaps in future you will attend the concerts, which you review in your capacity as music critic of the illustrious Guardian newspaper. Had you done so on this occasion, you might have been able to conceal your considerable lack of aural ability from your unfortunate and ill-served readers.

Yours sincerely

Terry Johns

"A luscious extravagance of cream silk."

LETTERS, LINES AND SPACES

OUR WEDDING TOOK PLACE IN EDINBURGH, IN JUNE 1973.

KARIN'S PARENTS, JACK AND ANNA, HAD BEEN PROPRIETORS OF "BRUCE'S" FAMOUS BAKERY IN THE CITY FOR MORE THAN TWENTY YEARS.

Mr. Ben Thomas

8 Ash Close
New Malden
Surrey

12th July 1973

Dear Ben

We were so sorry you couldn't manage to come to Edinburgh, and that you missed our wonderful day. We were married in St. Stephen's Church, which is just across the road from Bruce's bakery, famous in the City for its traditional Scottish baking, and as purveyor of "afternoon dainties" to genteel Lothian ladies.

Jack made us a scrumptious wedding cake, and endowed me with his beautiful and only daughter, who blinded the family and congregation with tears of joy and a luscious extravagance of cream silk, designed and made by a friend and theatrical costumier. The whole day was a wonderful celebration of new family and old friends, enriched with salmon, venison, champagne, malt whisky, and regency splendour.

We posed for photographs in front of the hotel in the June sunshine between showers of confetti, warm Edinburgh rain, and skilful enchanting from our visiting piper, splendid in full ceremonial tartan, while the city, restless all around us with tourists, was limbering up for another international festival.

Thanks for trying so hard to get to Edinburgh. I know how difficult these things can be.

LETTERS, LINES AND SPACES

Jim Brown was obliged to stay reluctantly in London to do some recordings on that weekend, in order to placate a fixer who was very angry with me for getting married and for inviting so many horn players to Edinburgh on his "big film" recording day.

When we do work for him, he's no doubt angry with us for taking ninety per cent of his fee!

Good Luck

Drac

LETTERS, LINES AND SPACES

THERE ARE MANY JEWISH PLAYERS IN THE ORCHESTRAS OF THE WORLD, AND SEVERAL THAT ARE SURVIVORS OF THE NAZI DEATH CAMPS. WHAT THEY ENDURED IN THOSE PLACES, AND THE CONSEQUENCES FOR THE REMAINDER OF THEIR LIVES IS BEYOND COMPREHENSION.

Dear Bob

When we left the Greyhounds at Los Angeles this morning, strewn with beer bottles, broken biscuits and orange peel, they had been home from home for us, for nearly a month, but finally here we are airborne and headed for London, puffed up and pickled in American generosity.

The RPO is a home for the homeless it seems to me. One of the violinists, Stefan Schwartz, spoke to me for the first time yesterday while we were waiting to go on the platform. I had wondered why he spent so much time alone and hardly spoke to anyone. I noticed him impatient for the arrival of food on aeroplanes, which he devours to the last crumb, licking his fingers and begging discarded scraps from his neighbours, most of whom proffer them without the slightest comment. The poor man spent most of the war at the camp at Auschwitz but never discusses it with anyone, beyond saying that the German guards had allowed him to keep his violin, because it suited them to have occasional entertainment and that they were too artless and insensible to know the value of it. He always remains apart from the other Jews who travel together, breaking off from their recreational quarrelling only to smile good morning.

I must say I feel homeless myself at times in the middle of all this, so I'll be going straight from Heathrow to Aberdare where God still goes to band practise on Sunday mornings to listen to some real music, played only for the love of it, and to warm himself by the tortoise stove and get a break from the cold war.

LETTERS, LINES AND SPACES

I feel the need of a change of pace and some respite from the paraphernalia of professional music.

Edinburgh is next and is always different. You will enjoy it immensely.

The atmosphere is unique and the city is beautifully Georgian, festive and Scottish. I took the liberty of making some "jazz plans" for us I hope you won't mind. I have to play some rehearsals and two concerts with the LSO, which should finish by 9.30 and not interfere with anything. I can hardly wait for this I've not heard a note of jazz in America, my morning whistlings for a month being only Schubert and Charles Ives.

Thank you for asking me to play at the club. When will you open? I would prefer to appear with someone else, only because I don't have my own group. You could ask Kenny Wheeler or Graham Collier. They both have material with french horn features that we've done before.

After band practice on Sunday I'll go to the Boot Hotel. I'm sure to find your father there all ex-constabulary and lambs wool. We always have lovely chats and a laugh, guzzling that Symond's bitter.

Good luck with the opening when it comes. I have only American coins in my pocket. When I get some British ones I'll telephone.

Yours Ever Terry

P.S.   The Hollywood Bowl was all I had imagined it would be – I saw fireflies for the first time and sent Bert Merret a postcard.

LETTERS, LINES AND SPACES

BRITISH ORCHESTRAS HAVE AT VARIOUS TIMES, BEEN TAKEN TO THE EDGE OF BANKRUPTCY BY THE FINANCIAL DEMANDS OF CONDUCTORS AND THE ACTIVITIES OF THEIR INTERNATIONAL AGENTS, BUT THE PAINS THAT HAVE BEEN TAKEN TO MEET THEIR OTHER DEMANDS, HAVE EXACTED A HUMAN COST WHICH HAS NOT INSPIRED SO MUCH PUBLIC DISCUSSION.

I BOUGHT A VINYL COPY OF THE RECORDING REFERRED TO IN THIS LETTER FOR 50P IN A CHARITY SHOP IN EDINBURGH IN 1992

Mr. Pat O'Brian
Theo Connelly
Fine Instruments
DUBLIN

8 Ash Close
New Malden
Surrey

18th October 1974

Dear Pat

Just returned with the downcast and destitute RPO from the upholstered opulence of Geneva where I had the duty and privilege of hearing Cecil James's RPO swansong, which was beautiful bassoon playing of the highest order, that rendered everybody speechless and bewildered. An extraordinary event, considering that he's been sacked, along with the leader, and two other eminent and brilliant players who I don't think you know. Another three violinists resigned in protest at the sackings.

The grisly end of their association with the RPO came at Abbey Road, during the orchestra's brave attempt to record "Scheherazade", which was interrupted constantly, by acrimonious board meetings in the recording booth, and the Teutonic tantrums of great maestro Kempe, the most dramatic of which came when Cecil informed the Maestro that he couldn't " play the bloody piece", and neither could his "Uncle Fred". (Fred James was first bassoon at the Queen's Hall with Henry Wood I think.) Anyway, the mere mention of "Uncle Fred" was for some reason, enough to send the Maestro into hyperventilation and mandibular paralysis, at which point, everyone, having been ordered out of the studio, went to the pub, including Cecil who couldn't "understand what all the fuss was about". He and the others weren't sacked until the next day when we all went back and had managed to salvage the recording.

All this mayhem happened because Kempe detests recording as you know, and the board, having spent months persuading him to record this Scheherazade for the good of the orchestra, are now having to sack their own colleagues, some of the finest players in the country, in order to placate him!! Everyone's blaming Uncle Fred of course, with typical RPO humour and resolve.

How's the violin trade? How is Dublin? I would love to come and see you. London is much the same, and the orchestra stumbles on, across Europe and half the World, with few friends and no money, dodging the bullets, with only the deficit intact, but it's great to be a part of it still, despite everything, and good to be back in one piece.

The streets are deserted on this Sunday morning, but for fallen leaves, and the scent of wood smoke from the allotment that sharpens my appetite for breakfast. The days are shortening, but this time at home that allows me to get acquainted with myself again is precious. I'm not entirely sure who or what I become during long orchestral tours, but I'm certainly changed by solitary, daily inventories in hotel rooms, and those reluctant rituals of boarding the airport bus and the evening Beethoven.

When I'm alone, which is now the rarest of events, I do feel like a stranger to myself and I long for a change of some kind.

Before the tour I did a few days work for RCA Victor with Charles Gerhardt. We recorded "The Sea Hawk" and a lot of classic Hollywood stuff in five or six sessions. Playing with that orchestra always makes me feel restless. Maybe it's the wads of cash they give you the minute you've finished. But more importantly, the sound of the orchestra, especially the strings is what every musician needs, like a warm coat in winter.

To add to my discomfort, Sid Sax has called me a couple of times recently, offering me dozens of recording sessions with the orchestra, and he was on the telephone for a long time, trying to persuade me to abandon the RPO for a life in the studios. I must say I'm very tempted. Things are a little better in the orchestra since the Union loan relieved the deficit, and getting paid almost every month makes such a difference to the atmosphere, but the Scheherazade affair depressed me and I'm tired of constantly fighting for survival now. The excitement is wearing thin.

Chuck Gerhardt is an unique musician and person, and lives a million miles from the childishness and self-destruction I've almost grown used to.

In the fifties, he was seconded to the Toscanini household to become RCA's liaison with their most important artist and since he's been in England he's produced hundreds of sessions with Barbirolli, Boult, Horenstein, and Stokowski, and many that he conducted himself. He doesn't seem to hold any personal ambition for fame or money and he won't conduct in public. He just lives in the recording studio making these wonderful records for RCA. The National Philharmonic is his brainchild, and Sid Sax keeps it full of leaders ex leaders, and top players simply because everybody wants to play in it, and the Americans want to use it for their films.

As you can tell, I've all but decided to cross over. Since you left for Ireland, Jim Brown and a few others have gone. It's getting lonely here.

Do you sell lots of violins and cellos? Is your mother overjoyed that you are in Dublin again? She'll be singing on Saturday nights now and lovelier than ever! Everyone asks me to send you best wishes. Please write with all your Irish humour and good news.

LETTERS, LINES AND SPACES

Yours ever

Drac

P.S. When Cecil was in the Philharmonia, Walter Legge raised some sponsorship for them, from the Maharajah of Mysore. Cecil used to call them the Mysore Legge concerts, usually in exalted company and with his perfect poker face.

"She's as beautiful as her mother"

LETTERS, LINES AND SPACES

OUR DAUGHTER SALLY-ANN WAS BORN AT KINGSTON HOSPITAL IN AUGUST 1974

Dr Walter Murfin
Glaslyn
TYWYN
Merionethshire

65 Hook Road
Surbiton
Surrey

August 1974

Dear Wally

You were right! You said we would have a girl, and that Karin might have a long labour, so full marks for intuition and obstetrics. After hours of pacing the hospital corridors, I was present at the birth and I shall never forget it. Thank you for insisting that I should be there. I had felt so squeamish about it beforehand, but the beauty of it all and the colours and everything were breathtaking.

How can a baby's crying sound so heavenly? How could I think of missing such a thing! And thank you for all the proxy doctoring and squalid uplifting humour. I did not feel even the slightest bit sick, so the staff were able to get on with their job without having to mop the floors after me!

We have called her Sally-Ann. She is as beautiful as her mother, and together in the hospital they made a picture like nothing I have ever seen. Come to London soon, and we can meet like the last time and wander around, jawing and catching up with one another.

Love and great joy from the three of us!

Drac.

LETTERS, LINES AND SPACES

PS We named her, by pure chance, after my grandmother, who died a long time before I was born. I had not known her name was Sally-Ann! My father was surprised and delighted!

LETTERS, LINES AND SPACES

HENRY MANCINI WAS BROUGHT UP IN CLEVELAND OHIO, WHERE HIS FATHER WAS A STEEL WORKER. AFTER THE WAR, HE WAS PIANIST AND ARRANGER FOR THE GLENN MILLER ORCHESTRA. HE ENJOYED NOTHING BETTER THAN THE COMPANY OF ORDINARY, WORKING MUSICIANS.

The Garden
"Crooked Billet"
Wimbledon

5th September 1975

Dear Ben

I was sorry and irritated when I missed you at Lime Grove last week. I did telephone in the evening, but was rendered speechless by your ansaphone.

How is Maggie? She looked well certainly when I saw her on television. I watched "Crossroads" to see her especially, and began to enjoy the programme – the escapism and the liberating safety of routine existence in one familiar place. The madhouse of London and commercial music is taking its toll on me right now.

Since I saw you I was at the Palace Hotel in Gstadt at a party given by Lew Grade, to launch the film 'Revenge of the Pink Panther'. We were there as the Henry Mancini orchestra to play the "panther" tune and a couple of numbers for Julie Andrews before dinner, which was a mountain of shellfish, char-broiled veal and baked Alaska, all washed down with pink champagne (maybe commercial music isn't all that bad). The whole weekend was pink from the aeroplane at Gatwick, to the water in the swimming pool, and the carnations in the buttonholes of our pink DJs, but the air turned blue in the hotel lobby when we arrived, when it emerged that the band had been excluded from the party and accommodated in the little demi-pension in the town. Hank Mancini, without even asking us, had said at once and finally, that we wouldn't be playing a note unless the band was installed in the hotel and invited to the party.

LETTERS, LINES AND SPACES

Lew Grade's draped overcoat and monster cigar seemed to be strangely irrelevant and incongruous during his transmogrification from media mogul to mere mortal, and the progress of his facial expressions was a picture as he faced the prospect of hosting his million-dollar weekend party, without any music!!! So he relented, and it was all resolved perfectly for us, and for Sid Sax who was gripped by the terror of upsetting his multi million pound clients, and the staff and the bell boys ran around placating everybody, and carrying our instruments and luggage, while we moved in to our pink hotel rooms.

Julie Andrews sang a couple of numbers with the strings of the Suisse Romande and a couple of romantic little solos from yours truly. Derek Watkins, Kenny Wheeler and the band with Bobby Orr drumming, blew up a storm with Peter Gunn, and Tony Coe played the panther tune before we tucked in to our lobster and veal.

The Burtons arrived some time after dinner when the party was at full throttle and in a huge explosion of flash bulbs, which was all I could see for a minute or two afterwards. I had a notion that it was pink, which was probably imagined. The Guardian reporter said a day later that Mrs. B had been in tears because the photographers wouldn't let her go to the bathroom, but things calmed down a little later. Stars and celebrities were everywhere and I spoke to Peter Sellers for a while, albeit through alcoholic incoherence and frontier gibberish. Then I went off to find Jim Brown who I had last seen splashing around in the pink swimming pool. Jim and I, when we got to Gatwick next day, went straight to Downe House to rehearse the Tippet horn quartet with Alan Civil for the Prom the following evening. This was to be broadcast from the Round House in Camden Town in a new series of "alternative" proms devised by the BBC.

Despite our hangovers and limited rehearsal time the performance was surprisingly good. Alan Civil is a brilliant player, so different from Barry, and more relaxed about it all. Do you remember 1969 at Aldeburgh? I missed you that day too. We (The

LETTERS, LINES AND SPACES

Tuckwell Quartet) played the Tippet piece in a live broadcast from the little church in Snape, the fire having almost destroyed the Maltings.

It's a pity the round house hadn't burned to the ground. It's an atrocious venue for concerts – most uncomfortable backstage and the acoustics are better at Paddington Station.

We will catch up with each other one day. I wonder if you ever see Maggie with her working at Granada all the time so if you're on your own in the flat try the phone, you never know!

Yours ever

Drac

P.S. Burton was too heavily surrounded to speak to, but I have met him before. He's a real gent and I've always admired him, apart from his acting ability, for what he's achieved in his life from difficult beginnings. You and I narrowly escaped working for a living. You'd have been no good underground anyway. You can't go without a fag for ten minutes!

LETTERS, LINES AND SPACES

"Mexico City is a crazy place"

THE SUMMER OF 1976 WAS THE HOTTEST IN THE UK SINCE RECORDS BEGAN. IN JULY OF THAT YEAR, I PLAYED AS A GUEST OF THE PHILHARMONIA ORCHESTRA OF LONDON ON THEIR TOUR OF MEXICO.

Hotel del Prado
Guadalajara
Mexico

July 1976

Darling

We have reached Guadalajara at last!! We're nearly home now, so I hope this letter arrives before I do!

Mexico City is cooler than London today the weathermen say, but it is a crazy place where, at this time of year, the rain comes to refresh the city streets like a benediction every day at precisely four o'clock, and in the Playa Garibaldi in the evenings, there's a cacophony of umpteen mariachi bands that play different tunes simultaneously for hours, sounding like Charles Ives' wildest musical dreams.

The tour agent urged us not to give money to the people that beg in the streets, and after some thought his reasons became clear, but the situation for these people is terrible. There's a boy that eats fire to entertain the tourists and sleeps in a paraffin soaked old blanket in the porch of the cathedral, and the streets around about are populated with homeless children and thousands of rats that emerge after dark.

Yesterday we gave a concert at midday in a little village outside Oaxaca. The music was relayed through speakers, to the square outside the church and people came for miles, and didn't have to pay to listen. The local brass band entertained us after the concert, and because they'd only one little cantina in the village, packed meals had been brought from the hotel. Some of us sat on a wall outside the church while the local people handed the food around and sat down to talk. They are so gracious and kind despite the poverty that afflicts them. I will remember them when I want to complain that my coffee is cold.

I can't imagine what it's like to be pregnant in this weather. You are a hero! It will be cooler in September, and soon we will be four.

Love forever

Drac

LETTERS, LINES AND SPACES

"Dylan Eil Ton - Sea Son of the wave"

DYLAN BRUCE JOHNS WAS BORN IN KINGSTON HOSPITAL IN SEPTEMBER 1976

Dr Walter Murfin
Glaslyn
TYWYN
Merionethshire

65 Hook Road
Surbiton
Surrey

Dear Wally

You were right once again! It all happened so quickly! I rushed down from Wembley to Kingston hospital, to find that our new family member had already arrived!

After my morning of Bruckner, solemnity and piety, and an hour of subterranean, airless anxiety on the Bakerloo line, the maternity ward was filled with sunshine, smiling faces and the sounds of new life. One lady on the staff told me that every child she had helped into the world had given her the same pure joy and amazement, that twenty years as a midwife could never diminish. The warmth of her smile deepened my disappointment at not having arrived in time, remembering how beautiful and colourful Sally's birth was.

I do remember also, that but for your firm insistence, I might have missed that great event, simply through cowardice and haemophobia.

It's ten years since that night in Aberystwyth, when you delivered a baby at the hospital and you predicted that I would have children of my own one-day. I never imagined how wonderful it would be. Thank you for everything, and for your friendship of years. You always did enjoy helping people I know.

Karin's so happy to have a boy. We have named him Dylan -- It is an ancient Welsh name, from the "Mabinogion".

> "and straightaway he made for the sea. And when he reached the shore he became at once part of the sea, he partook of its nature, and he swam as fast as the swiftest fish. And for that reason he was called Dylan Eil Ton, Sea Son of the Wave."

Perhaps he'll be a sailor. That's a proper job, like a miner or even a doctor.   That'd be something.

Yours ever

Drac

LETTERS, LINES AND SPACES

ERIC ROGERS COMPOSED THE MUSIC FOR MOST OF THE "CARRY ON" FILMS, AND HE PROVIDED THE ARRANGEMENTS FOR THE STAGE SHOW OF LIONEL BART'S "OLIVER" AT THE "NEW THEATRE" IN ST. MARTIN'S LANE. I PLAYED IN THE ORCHESTRA THERE WHEN I WAS STILL A STUDENT, AND I MET HIM AGAIN IN THE EARLY SEVENTIES, WHEN HE HAD WRITTEN THE ARRANGEMENTS FOR "MERMAN SINGS MERMAN", WHICH WE RECORDED WITH THE GREAT LADY HERSELF, FOR DECCA RECORDS AND STANLEY BLACK.

ERIC LIVED CLOSE TO THE DENHAM FILM STUDIOS, AND REGARDED THE "SWAN" PUBLIC HOUSE IN THE VILLAGE AS HIS OWN. MUSICIANS VISITING THE STUDIOS WERE NEVER ALLOWED TO PAY FOR THEIR OWN DRINKS.

THE LONDON SYMPHONY ORCHESTRA PROVIDED SOUNDTRACKS FOR "THINGS TO COME", "HENRY V", "THE MAN WHO KNEW TOO MUCH", "DANGEROUS MOONLIGHT", "THE MUSIC LOVERS", AND MANY MORE.

IN 1977 THE ORCHESTRA RETURNED TO THE FILM STUDIO, IN A FILM THAT WAS TO CHANGE THE COURSE OF CINEMA HISTORY.

Mr. Pat O'Brien
Theo Connelly
Fine Instruments
DUBLIN

65 Hook Road
Surbiton
Surrey

18th March 1977

Dear Pat

How is Dublin's fair city?

Knowing you as I do I'm certain that you thank God every day for Ireland, and to be there and home again. What a blessing it is for your mother to have her family together once more!

LETTERS, LINES AND SPACES

I am so grateful that my own family is together more often, now that I'm freelancing here in London, and every day, for a little while at least, I can be with them, instead of hurtling across the Atlantic Ocean, or sitting on a Greyhound bus ten thousand miles from home.

It's a wonderful stroke of fortune, that almost every musician in the World wants to come to London now, so I am able to play for Giulini and Barry White on the same day, without leaving the city, or I can take the train out to Denham as I did last week, to play with the LSO, who are venturing into the world of the cinema again.

I stepped down from the early morning train on the first day and there on the platform was Harry Nathan!

He showed me to a footpath that led us away from the busy road, across some open farmland and up to the studio. What a joy it was, just a few miles from London, to hear the birds singing in the hedgerows, and to feel grass under my feet for a while.

The spring air and the walk gave us a lovely start to the day, and almost an hour before the recording was due to begin, still touched by country quietude, I sat down in the studio to share Harry's kichel cookies and coffee.

"It's some kind of space film", Harry said, shrugging and munching. "I don't know -- Battle for the Stars, or something".

As the musicians and Americans arrived, the conversation we overheard was about a plan for eight of these films ("Star Wars" it's called) that would take thirty years to make, and people were saying that a million pounds had already been spent on the sessions for this one.

LETTERS, LINES AND SPACES

Besides a huge orchestra, there was a posse of technical people that included Ernie "eyeshade" of course, with his team of copyists, and Lionel Newman, who supervised everything and conducted some of the rehearsals.

John Williams' orchestral writing is better than ever! This score, particularly the way he uses the brass and horns, seems to add another dimension to the film, and with six horns we were able to get across the rich orchestration without strain or overblowing, and we got the wide-open sound that he wanted.

The opening sequence is a big Hollywood fanfare that dissolves into some brilliant Waltonesque music, and a dramatic pursuit in space, of the Rebel blockade-runner, by the immense Star Destroyer of the Evil Galactic Empire.

The mixture of music and effects, draws you right in to the drama of war in deep space. It had an astonishing effect on everyone in the studio, and when the lights went up after the first playback, there was a spontaneous burst of applause, that I can't remember happening at any film recording before.

The LSO has enjoyed a golden era since Previn came here to remind them, what a great orchestra they are, and people have a new transatlantic confidence to match. It's hard to imagine them getting over-enthusiastic about anything, but there was a real excitement in the studio that lasted all week.

At one point, George Lucas got so excited, he called his pal Spielberg in Hollywood, to let him hear the opening fanfare through the telephone, and during playbacks, with the studio in darkness, the orchestra was cheering for the "Jedi", and booing the evil "Darth Vader", just like the kids in the "Rex" cinema in Aberdare!! – George was delighted of course—to have had an early preview! So there was a tremendous buzz going around as we headed off to "The Swan" to get lunch.

LETTERS, LINES AND SPACES

Eric Rogers was in the pub when we arrived. -- I should have known!! -- And within minutes there was not an inch of elbowroom in the bar, and some people were standing outside on the green.

Not many of the LSO players had encountered Eric before, so they didn't know that they weren't allowed to pay for any of their own drinks, and most were shocked to silence and acquiescence by his loudness and generosity, that went into overdrive when someone told him that Maurice Murphy had just completed his first session with the LSO as principal trumpet.

Maurice was forced to drink Veuve Clicquot with his Ploughman's lunch!!

It really turned out to be quite a day, and there was relief and a lot of smiling faces in the studio, when we finished playing at 5 30.
Harry and I hitched a ride back into London with Jack Steadman, and Harry sat in the back of the car, still munching and talking about the film music that he remembered recording at Denham.

He played on "Vertigo" in 1958, with Bernard Herrmann, when I was still at school. That got me thinking about the smoky old "Palace" cinema in Hirwaun, where I first heard the soundtracks of the "Big Country" and the "Vikings". I was enthralled by the sound of those orchestral horns – reaching out, and shining like a broad highway to somewhere or other – I followed it all the way to Denham!

What a thought – "We are the dreamers of dreams".

You and your family have your dream at last, and the tenacity and self-belief of our old RPO friends has finally brought them some real hope. All this change for the better makes me feel so good, but I miss you all the same, and I often think about your Irish humour and optimism that helped to keep us all going in those dark days.

LETTERS, LINES AND SPACES

Karin loves and personifies motherhood, and has thrived on London life for a long time. The children reflect her joy and delight.

My musical life could not be better now, mainly because I'm working with arrangers or composers and I don't see many "conductors". I'm still depressed at the thought of one walking in to a rehearsal, with Beethoven under his arm and a professional smile on his face, like the vicar on the doorstep.

You will love this film!

Write soon with Dublin jokes and violin experiences.

Yours ever

Drac

LETTERS, LINES AND SPACES

ON THE 9TH OF NOVEMBER 1978, I WAS ASKED TO PRODUCE A
CONCERT, "A GARLAND FOR DYLAN THOMAS", THAT WAS GIVEN
AT THE WEMBLEY CONFERENCE CENTRE TO MARK THE 25TH
ANNIVERSARY OF THE POET'S DEATH IN NEW YORK. LONDON'S
"CAPITAL RADIO" STATION BROADCAST THE EVENT.

BEN THOMAS, WHO WAS SUFFERING FROM CANCER, LAY DYING
IN THE LONDON HOSPITAL AT WHITECHAPEL. HE DIED A FEW
DAYS LATER.

8 Ash Close
New Malden
Surrey

1st November 1978

Dear Wally

I have fifteen minutes to write this, plus probable lateness of my airport taxi, so this is in
great haste and distress to tell you that Ben's condition has worsened considerably
since you were at the hospital.

When I saw him yesterday, he was breathing with oxygen and only with great difficulty.
Some of Bob Sharples band from Opportunity Knocks turned up with a case of beer,
which failed to tempt him for a second, and when I left, one or two bottles had been
opened in a very strained, trying to be cheerful atmosphere...

I had to leave to attend a meeting with Gerry O'Reilly at Capital radio that will broadcast
"A Garland for Dylan Thomas", on Nov. 9th. Ben won't be there that's for sure. I feel
terrible now -- horribly confused and anxious, and helpless but I keep telling myself it
will be a great Welsh night and maybe Ben will be able hear the broadcast. He helped
me such a lot with it in the early stages, with ideas for the programme and introducing
me to people.

LETTERS, LINES AND SPACES

Neil Kinnock and Glenys will be there, Dannie Abse will be reading Dylan's poems, and some of his own, and Stan Tracey's jazz suite "Under. Milk Wood" with Donald Houston will form the second half.

If by any chance you are able to come, phone me and I'll arrange tickets for you.

What a calamity this is. Everyone is subdued and lost for words.

Tal Thomas arrived at the hospital as I was leaving (Ben has as many doctors among his friends as are in attendance I'm sure). Tal told me that there is in effect no hope at all of a recovery, surgery being ruled out because of the location of the tumor. That was all the conversation that passed between us and I hadn't seen him for two or three years. A cheerful little Cockney lady with an old raincoat, tied around with string sold me an "Evening Standard" on the steps of the hospital and I was late for Gerry O'Reilly. I couldn't' get a taxi in the hosing rain, and the meeting didn't seem to be important in the slightest.

I hope you can manage to come. We'll all need to be together I think.

Ever

 Drac

LETTERS, LINES AND SPACES

8 Ash Close
New Malden
Surrey

Dear Wally

It's all over at last and I have an awful desolate feeling.

Thank you for your letter. I can understand perfectly why you were not able to come to Morriston. My last few weeks experience has shown me what a dedicated life doctors lead. The ones at the London hospital did so much to make Ben comfortable through those last days.

The concert went well and was well attended. Michael Aspel who introduced it all, and showed a remarkable knowledge of Dylan's poetry, wrote to us to say how much he had enjoyed the evening. Here are a few photographs and a tape from the radio station.

The recording won't of course convey to you the poignancy of the atmosphere in the hall. Some people had come, I think, straight to the concert from the hospital. Bill Mathias' songs," Fields of Praise", were beautifully sung by Ken Bowen with Bill at the piano. But there is, as you will hear, a lot of extraneous noise on the recording.

The high point I felt was the Stravinsky "In Memoriam". The middle movement brought the audience to somewhere beyond silence, with the beauty of the music, the poetry, and the thought of Ben lying in the hospital.

Stan Tracey's jazz suite with the hilarity of "Under Milk Wood", brilliantly delivered by Donald Houston was exactly the release the audience needed for the second half. At that point I was hoping that Ben was able to hear the broadcast from his hospital bed.

LETTERS, LINES AND SPACES

After the concert we took almost all the tables at the Golden Bengal in Wembley to end a great evening and Kinnock kept everyone entertained, but the news of course of Ben's death inevitably was not long in coming.

The funeral was another reunion this time in the mud and relentless rain of Morriston. The singing of the male voice choir moved me so much that I could not participate. I just moved my lips and tried to hold myself together bizarrely by concentrating on Glyn Price who was in the pew in front of me. I had never seen him in a suit before, and the borrowed one he was wearing did not fit him and was a strange indeterminate colour.

Ben's father Bert was beside himself and wept all through the oration. He had lost his wife, his daughter and now this. It was heart rending. Margaret sat beside him, serenely beautiful. Through the whole service, I couldn't take my eyes off her, knowing how fiercely she loved Ben, and wondering what was going through her mind.

Jerry Richards, with head in hands, was in floods of tears in the pub and as the afternoon wore on with people having to drive back to London, things got worse, and the rain never stopped. In the train next day I could think of nothing but Ben and when my feet touched the platform at Paddington I felt like a sailor home from the sea.
When we were boys, his only dream and ambition was to be a professional musician. I felt grateful that he had achieved that and I remembered him in the BBC club at Wood Lane drinking with Windsor Davis and Tommy Cooper. I remembered him playing on television with the National Youth Orchestra of Wales and at the Festival Hall with the Royal Philharmonic. His humour and love of life were an inspiration to everyone that knew him. He never lost gratitude for what he had been given. I felt enormously different on that station platform - just as if he had passed his gratitude on to me.

Yours ever

Drac

LETTERS, LINES AND SPACES

RONNIE HAZLEHURST COMPOSED THE WELL KNOWN THEMES AND INCIDENTAL MUSIC FOR MANY BBC TELEVISION PROGRAMMES, IN PARTICULAR COMEDIES SUCH AS "THE LAST OF THE SUMMER WINE", "YES MINISTER" AND THE "RISE AND FALL OF REGINALD PERRIN".

I JOINED THE TELEVISION ORCHESTRA AT RON'S INVITATION, IN 1976.

65 Hook Road
Surbiton
Surrey

6th April 1979

Dear Mum

Thanks for the parcel and for giving me a week to unwrap it, which should, be sufficient time, given the proper tools. I'll spend my birthday this year at Lime Grove studios, rehearsing for the Val Doonican show that goes out on Saturday the 14th with Burl Ives as the guest. I know you'll want to watch it. Did you see the last one?

I'm so comfortable and happy on live TV without petulant conductors, potential recording contracts and lost luggage. This is pure professionalism. The television orchestra ticks like a Swiss watch, shock proof and accurate to the millisecond and Ronnie Hazlehurst's arrangements and direction are flawless. Working on the "Two Ronnies" show is hilarious too. It does me a power of good. It's like being back in the RPO!

Life for me now is life in west London, spent between Lime Grove, Television centre and the television theatre. Paddington station is only a short distance too, so I will catch the two o'clock train to Cardiff on Monday the 16th after the morning session at Lime Grove. As promised, I should be with you before seven. I want to get an early train back

LETTERS, LINES AND SPACES

to London on Wednesday morning, only if Dad can drive me to Cardiff. I hope that you are both well, as are all of us here. The children are thriving and growing and Karin sends her love.

Terence

LETTERS, LINES AND SPACES

IN 1980, WHEN THE MUSICIANS' UNION WAS BEGINNING ITS DISPUTE WITH THE BBC, I WAS INVITED TO JOIN THE LONDON SYMPHONY ORCHESTRA, FOR WHOM THE FUTURE LOOKED BRIGHT, DESPITE THE ECONOMIC DIFFICULTIES FACED, BY THE COUNTRY AND OUR PROFESSION.

A TOUR OF JAPAN AND KOREA WITH THE GREAT SERGIU CELIBIDACHE WAS ONE THE MOST EXCITING OF MY MUSICAL LIFE. I WAS ASKED TO SHARE THE FIRST HORN DUTIES FOR THE TOUR WITH JIM BROWN AND WHEN WE RETURNED TO LONDON, I WAS TO GIVE THE BOARD MY DECISION. MY FATHER CELEBRATED HIS SEVENTIETH BIRTHDAY IN APRIL OF THAT YEAR.

Mr. Arthur Johns   65 Hook Road
86 Tramway   Surbiton
HIRWAUN   Surrey
Glamorgan

14th April 1980

Dear Dad

My birthday celebrations are over and done with and my bags are packed, so I can leave for Tokyo early in the morning. Nearly next door to us here is a grocery owned and run by a lovely Bangladeshi man called Jerry. He operates a taxi service as well as everything else, and often drives me to airports and stations, and he'll come and ring the doorbell an hour before we're due to leave just to make sure I'm vertical.

I can remember Uncle Tommy, tapping at the window to wake you at five o'clock on winter mornings, as I turned over in the warm bed, knowing I had hours to sleep before I had to get up for school. You were about forty then, and had another twenty-five years of work ahead of you. All those years underground never darkened your spirit. You are an amazing man and you have been a shining example to me of how to accept the less pleasant aspects of life and to be grateful for its pleasures and bonuses. On your birthday I'll be playing in my last concert with the L.S.O. in Japan before going to Korea, so I'm writing this now to make sure you get it before the big day. I'm sorry that I can't be there for the celebrations but I'll be coming down right after the tour at the beginning of May.

The L.S.O. has asked me to become a permanent member of the orchestra and they have given me a fortnight to think it over. I have their schedule on the desk and I don't mind telling you it's very tempting. There will be a major World tour in 1983 and the opening of the new Barbican hall in 1982. There will be a tour of Russia as well in1983 with Colin Davis and the sound track for Revenge of the Jedi, which is the new Star Wars film. I must say I feel very fortunate indeed, given the state of the profession at the moment, to have an opportunity like this.

The B.B.C.is squaring up for a very big confrontation with the Musicians' Union over a decision to disband five orchestras, and employment in films and television has diminished considerably, mainly due to the increasing use of synthesizers but also because the big named orchestras are taking on the American films now that government funding to the arts is being cut so drastically.

The future looks black for musicians at the moment and it seems as if I'll be involved in a strike soon that may affect the Proms. You will have to give me some advice about strikes; people are getting very heated over this.

Neil Kinnock was on the phone the other day; you'll remember he was in the Glamorgan youth choir and he and I have kept in touch regularly since then. He wanted to talk about the strike and asked if I was involved in any way. He was asking for you too and I told him you were coming up for seventy and how you'd said you never expected to live this long, considering your involvement in underground explosions strikes air raids, two World wars, and forty one years working at Tower colliery.

LETTERS, LINES AND SPACES

He said he doesn't believe that the miners' problems are over by any means, and that you are lucky to be away from it now, and he's usually right. He was right about the election certainly and said ominously that these Tories are a new breed like nothing we have ever seen before in this country.

I feel fortunate not to be directly threatened, for the present anyway, with the problems in the music profession and I feel strangely guilty about my good fortune at the same time.

But I really must not dwell on all this on your birthday. I wish I could be there to play Happy Birthday on the piano for you, but I can't so here's a tape of me playing it on the horn and the piano together, courtesy of modern technology and a mate of mine at C.B.S.

Have a great day when it comes.

Terence

P.S. I got you a subscription to National Geographic and a surprise that'll have to wait til May

BARRY BOOTH IS MY OLD FRIEND OF FORTY-FIVE YEARS, AND IN 1980 WAS MUSICAL DIRECTOR FOR THE ENTERTAINER ROLF HARRIS.

SERGIU CELIBIDACHE WAS ONE OF THE FINEST CONDUCTORS OF ALL TIME. HE WAS FAMOUSLY AVERSE TO STUDIO RECORDING; CONSEQUENTLY HIS NAME IS NOT AS FAMILIAR TO THE PUBLIC AS SOME OTHERS ARE.

HE BECAME CONDUCTOR OF THE BERLIN PHILHARMONIC AT THE END OF THE WAR, PRIOR TO VON KARAJAN'S APPOINTMENT.

LETTERS, LINES AND SPACES

Mr. Barry Booth
Mallinson Road
CLAPHAM
London

Korean Airlines
Tokyo to Seoul

28th April 1980

Dear Barry

I've just played ten concerts in Japan with the L.S.O. and Celbidache and we're en route for Korea. Thank you for your postcard I knew you would enjoy the Festival hall concert. I'm sorry we couldn't have got together afterwards.

Rite of spring and Daphnis and Chloe on the same programme makes a hell of a concert doesn't it? I wonder if it's ever been done before, and I certainly don't want to do it again for a while. The rehearsals were devastating, even though Mata is a perfect gentleman and makes everything as comfortable as possible.

Celibidache, by contrast conducts rehearsals in a way that is unique to him I think, taking a half-hour break every half hour and for at least six three hour sessions prior to every concert, which sounds exhausting when you put it like that, but is actually stimulating and exciting.

This entire trip has been exciting, even the travelling, and because the mood amongst the players is relaxed with a feeling of unique achievement that usually eludes an orchestra on tour.

The Korean stewardesses, all in silk sarongs are fussing over the passengers in the cabin, and I can feel the huge latent power of the aeroplane. There's a Japanese airliner up ahead of us. We'll take to the runway after him, and be off again to yet another country.

LETTERS, LINES AND SPACES

My feelings about performing, how and why we do it, even about music itself have been completely rearranged by these concerts with Celibidache.

In the middle of "Iberia" last night, after taking the platform feeling less than on top form, I felt as if the music had pervaded all my senses at once and dispersed my headache, nausea and homesickness.

I sat with the great man on the outward flight from London for an hour or so, listening as he told me why he would not make studio recordings and why he insisted on so much "preparation" for concerts. The preparation is for us, not for the music, he told me.

Music, properly understood, is a "cosmic event", he insists and the long preparation is needed to learn to perceive and perform it in a different way, to be free from negative influences and to realize the irrelevance of criticism. We talked about the horn too, and he knew exactly what Dukas meant by " son d'echo", and that the solo in "The Sorcerer's Apprentice" was spoiled so often when it was played with a mute or handstopped when the player was using a modern instrument, not capable of producing what the composer was asking for. The horn is also, he says, one of the instruments worst affected by studio recording techniques, because of its unique reflected sound.

I wanted to ask him about his own music.

"You are a composer", I said. "Of course", he replied. "A musician makes music".

Celibidache is a fascinating man and at the same time I believe he is sincere when he says he is "no one special". He has humility and humour, and he's very interested in people, particularly if they are in his orchestra.

"Why do they call you Drac ", he asked me eventually, and with a little anger in his voice, as if he were concerned in some way for my dignity. I explained the origin of the nickname, how it derived from my student days when I was seldom seen in the hours of daylight, only after dark and dressed in tails. As I entered the realms of vampirology he cut me off abruptly.

"Don't tell me about vampires!" he barked, "I was born in Transylvania!"

I don't find him to be in the least bit frightening, though I'm sure others do. The growling, I interpret as a kind of frustration with the mundane business of living in hotels and aeroplanes. He is at perfect ease with the players and the porters-- it's the users and sycophants that he is uncomfortable with and detects instantly. You would get on famously with him I'm sure.

How is the lovely family? How's Rolf on Saturday? Have you heard anything officially from the B.B.C. about the dispute? I hope the B.B.C. don't get what they want, it would be disaster for the profession but I'd certainly love to come and play in the band again when things settle down although it might be more difficult for me in future. The L.S.O. want me to join them permanently, and I have all but decided to accept. It's too good to miss really so far as the music is concerned, my only objection being the large amount of touring on the schedule. I've hardly been out of London in the last ten years as you know and the children are still so young. I feel as if I should be at home as much as I can be but Karin understands "show business" of course and she knows that the future certainly looks bleak for the studios and T.V.

We have two more concerts in Seoul to end the tour. We'll play Tippet's Dances from "Midsummer Marriage". Debussy's "Iberia". Mussorgsky, "Pictures from an Exhibition, Kodaly "Dances from Galanta", Ravel's Mother Goose, and the first symphony of Brahms.

Celibidache has rehearsed and conducted every note of this music, faultlessly and without the use of a score for any of it. The concerts have been momentous and some of the older men say they have not heard the L.S.O. sound like this for many years.

LETTERS, LINES AND SPACES

I've never seen or heard anything remotely like it and I never expect to again. We have some more concerts with him later in the year. I hope you will be able to come.

I'll be going to Wales in a few days to visit my father who had his seventieth birthday yesterday. He always watches Rolf on Saturday with his nephew and nieces and often asks after you. He told me that he had never expected to live this long and that he only regrets having worried about anything. There's a lesson for all of us!!

We are cruising comfortably now, in the bright morning sky. Glasses are tinkling and the trombones are bellowing with laughter at the back of the cabin. Korea here we come!!

Willie Lang tells me that dog meat is delicious if it's top quality and cooked with artistry. Non cave canem - Arrivederci Fido!

Good luck and regards to Rolf and the band.

Drac

LETTERS, LINES AND SPACES

THE MUSIC OF KARL JENKINS IS PERFORMED MORE WIDELY IN THE WORLD, THAN THAT OF ANY LIVING COMPOSER. WHEN WE WERE SCHOOLBOYS, HE AND I PLAYED IN THE NATIONAL YOUTH ORCHESTRA OF WALES TOGETHER.

IN NOVEMBER 1980, AT THE ROYAL FESTIVAL HALL IN LONDON, THE LSO GAVE A CONCERT TO CELEBRATE THE 80TH BIRTHDAY OF AARON COPELAND, CONDUCTED BY THE COMPOSER.

65 Hook Road
Surbiton
Surrey

Dear Karl

I'm sure you know Copland's "Quiet City"? It has no horns in the score, so I was able to listen to it at this morning's rehearsal with the composer conducting the LSO and Maurice Murphy playing the solo trumpet part. I was the only person in this huge auditorium in the centre of London, which seemed like a perfect situation for listening to this music. What a beautiful and evocative piece it is and how skilfully he writes for instruments. He knows precisely the register where they sound best, and exactly what orchestral colour the music requires. He's a very good conductor too, like you, without a lot of fuss and without talking any more than is necessary. I'm enjoying myself immensely here.

We're rehearsing at the Festival hall for Copland's eightieth birthday concert which will take place tonight and I'm sitting backstage waiting to rehearse "El Salon Mexico", "Billy the Kid' and the clarinet concerto with Jack Brymer as the soloist.

There's nobody and nothing behind here with me, except for flight cases with strewn around playing cards and loose change from the poker game that goes on every day, travelling from hall to hall, from country to country, and coach to airport bar.

LETTERS, LINES AND SPACES

Dimitroff Pashanko, a Romanian bass player with an artificial leg and a permanent cigar, who's been in the orchestra for more than thirty years, plays cards at every opportunity in the day and when on tour, for half the night. Playing stud poker stops the "tunes flying around" inside his head, he says and I must say, I sometimes struggle to quieten my own thoughts, most especially when I'm away from home.

Composers live constantly with sounds and notes and chords running around in the brain don't they? I know this from my own efforts at composition, which cause me a lot of distress, when I can't get any peace to work, or access to a piano, and relief comes only when the notes appear on paper.

It's difficult for me to understand how you work with this and with the isolation and self-discipline that it exacts from you, when music making for me almost always involves other people, and, for an orchestral player is almost always an objective process.

That's why I feel most comfortable playing with those conductors who are composers, and particularly so when they conduct their own music. This really is music making from the inside, which is where I want to be, and playing with this orchestra has given me so many opportunities to play with composers conducting.

Barry Tuckwell brought me here first when I was barely twenty and I played in a famous performance of the "War Requiem" conducted by Britten himself. Since then I've played with Leonard Bernstein, Walton, Michael Tippet, Arthur Bliss and lots of film composers, including John Williams and Previn of course, who has taught me so much. He would talk about music day and night if he could.

I have conducted my own music too, once or twice, with studio orchestras and brass bands, and it is the best thing I have experienced personally so far, so I understand what it is that motivates you, but I don't have the necessary courage or self reliance to be a proper composer.

LETTERS, LINES AND SPACES

11.13 Waterloo to Surbiton

It's been a very long exhilarating day but I'm able to relax at last and write a little, which will keep me from falling asleep on this train, the consequence of which can be an unplanned visit to Guildford or even Portsmouth so I'll open the window a little and hope to see a taxi on the rank when I get to Surbiton.

This afternoon I went up to Boosey & Hawkes in Regent Street to see their Copeland birthday exhibition, and to buy a miniature score of his "short symphony", hoping that he would sign it for me, which he did gladly and modestly in his dressing room before the concert.

Quiet City, Copeland, and all the music we played today have made an unusual impression on me. Music like this puts reality into a different perspective. It's so exciting and encouraging; it makes me want to write again but I need to eat and feed my family and I thrive in orchestras and strongly need their companionship and humour. Here we go!! Surbiton next stop. I'll be coming back to London in a few hours on the 8.15 train.

Good luck

Drac

LETTERS, LINES AND SPACES

IN AUGUST 1984, I ARRANGED THE MUSIC FOR THE FINAL HYMN OF THE MEMORIAL SERVICE FOR RICHARD BURTON C.B.E. AT THE ROYAL PARISH CHURCH OF ST. MARTIN-IN-THE-FIELDS, IN LONDON. THE WORK SCHEDULE OF THE LSO WAS AS CONGESTED AS EVER.

Mr. Bob Jones   65 Hook Road
Churchill's Club   Surbiton
CARDIFF   Surrey

                                               1st September 1984

Dear Bob

How's life underground? I have that picture of you behind the bar at Churchill's in my mind's eye- and the beguiling sound of the jazz spinning in my brain—that ride cymbal and bass, bumping along like an underground train. I'm sorry; I am a rotten bastard for not having written to you for so long.

Our tour seemed to last six months but it lasted, in fact only six weeks and, despite visits to New York, Los Angeles and Chicago, I heard no jazz at all for the whole time we were away—only Mahler, Mozart and Bartok who's sounds I could not evict from my head in between concerts and countries and who, joined forces, (mostly in the mornings) with unintelligible airport tannoys, muzak, and screaming jet engines to assault my senses, intensifying my homesickness, self pity, gratuitous racism, and xenophobia.

Homecoming was sweet but, there was very little respite before leaving again, and the two or three days I had set aside for writing were tied up in loose ends and repacked before you could say Edinburgh, with the consequence that my music for Burton's memorial service on the 30th of August was nowhere near finished. So having written some of it on the train journey to Edinburgh, we gave a concert in the Usher hall on the previous night with Rafael Kubelik, after which Maurice Murphy and I took the midnight sleeper back to London, with only the six-hour journey within which to finish the job. Maurice took the top bunk, whilst my manuscript, and I occupied the lower one, and we got on with it.

I had been asked to make a choir and organ arrangement for the Rhos Cwmtawe choir and to compose a solo obbligato trumpet part for the last verse of the "Battle Hymn of the Republic", that was to be the final hymn of the service as the actor had himself requested.

The arrangement was finished and the choral and organ parts copied and checked and only the trumpet solo remained to be done. Clattering through the night on the train, the piece began to take shape, and I passed the manuscript to Maurice in the bunk above for approval from time to time.

We arrived at King's cross at a very early hour, and stood for a while, on the arrival platform, unshaven and dazed, amid all the station staff, and their morning sweeping and trundling. My crumpled up tail suit and I, got to sleepy Surbiton an hour or so later with no time for breakfast, just a shave and a change of clothes. Karin, after reassuring and tie straightening for me, made herself ready and delectable instantly, and drove us both to London for the service.

Trafalgar Square was crammed with hundreds of people who had waited since early morning for the arrival of the stars and celebrities; the traffic had all but stopped, and police and news cameramen jostled for vantage points on the steps of the church.
Karin and Shirley stood in the queue with the privileged and invited, to take their seats in the congregation, while Maurice and I darted into the "Welsh Harp" in Chandos Place. We stopped to draw breath, for the first time for hours it seemed, savouring the aromas of yeast and hops and furniture polish of the mid-morning pub, and a few

minutes later we were standing in the chilled reverence of the church, for a few softly spoken words and instructions that had to serve as a rehearsal.

Robert Hardy, who was in charge of the arrangements for the service, and at whose invitation I had arranged the hymn, introduced us to John Gielgud, Paul Scofield and Emlyn Williams as if WE were people of some importance, which, after twenty something years of the relative anonymity of orchestral life came as something of a surprise and pleasure to us both, and at which point I was suddenly overwhelmed by a sense of great relief in the knowledge that the music had been finished in time.

The events of the previous day, combined with White Label Worthington with no breakfast, the solemnity of the occasion and my near sleepless night were beginning to make their effect.

The service was more moving than you could ever imagine. The sounds in the church, of the harp, of Welsh voices and Welsh hymns, English thespian oratory and eloquence, and finally the majestic sound of Maurice's trumpet rising to the buttresses above the choir, all combined to drain away my natural defences and restraints and I found myself tearful and unable to speak for a while, though comfortably hidden by the organ console from the main part of the congregation.

Later on at the Savoy hotel, my consciousness restored, from the other worldliness of night trains and Celtic necromancy, I began to breathe normally again and to reflect that somehow I had been plunged into another world of creation, and I had given more of myself to this important event, (which was unlike anything I had done before), than I had ever given to any orchestra or conductor. Orchestral life seems to consist of single unrelated experiences and encounters, and the path that I had followed here had been overgrown with doubts and littered with the debris of material things. I seem to have spent my life on the opposite shore, looking across to sunlit lands, by "lonely sea breakers", listening to jazz after a symphony concert in a strange city, or in an hotel room, longing for home, but there on that summer afternoon, at last I felt safe. I felt that I had been going the right way all along, and I wondered if this was to be the beginning of something entirely new for me.

The reception passed smoothly, music, being conspicuous by its absence and there was only the murmuring of lowered voices, and gentle tinkling of ice cubes on glass, to wile away the afternoon and ease me gently back to normality.

I spent an hour or so, in the company of Graham Jenkins, Richard's brother, a dynamic and very sociable Welshman, who was, for some reason, intensely interested in me and my background and became very busy through the afternoon, introducing me to people he thought I should like to meet. He eventually left our company for a while, only to return with pewter pint tankards for our champagne, to " make things easier for the poor waiters", and his celebrated sister-in law, herself, who, wanted to thank me "personally" for the music. As she spoke, I couldn't help thinking about her as Maggie Pollitt, Martha, Cleopatra, and all her alter egos that I remembered from smoky Saturday afternoons in the Rex cinema in, Aberdare.

She took me completely by surprise and her, charm and refinement kept pulling me back to the reality and reverence in the room, reminding me what this day and this occasion meant to her, and that actors and musicians are real people, and have real feelings too besides the ones they sell to the public.

Enough of high society, except to tell you that we were listed in the Court and Social column of the "Times" next day, by which my mother was rendered coy and embarrassed and complained about having to tell everybody. Father was totally indifferent.

LETTERS, LINES AND SPACES

It will be good to see you again. How are things at Churchill's? I often lust for the louche, licentious life and the sound of an old piano, decorated with beer glasses. I hope the smoke never clears and the music never stops.

Do you ever visit the world? -- Let's go up to Aberdare and have a pint in "The Boot". It'll be like old times. I'll blindfold you like a pit pony against the daylight in case you get to like it and forget your calling. I am a worthless worm for not writing until now but I know you will forgive me.

I'll come to Cardiff to see you in October when the music festivals are all done with and there are autumn leaves in Cathedral road.

Yours as ever

Terry J

LETTERS, LINES AND SPACES

IN 1983, THE LSO UNDERTOOK AN EXTENSIVE TOUR OF AMERICA, JAPAN, AUSTRALIA, AND THE FAR EAST.

Hilton
Hawaiian Village
Honolulu

July 1983

Dear Martin

I'm sitting under a palm tree looking out to sea and there are sand grains between my toes. The climate here is perfect, like paradise, there's a three masted schooner anchored in the bay, and in front of me on a bamboo table I have an outrageous drink made with white rum and a whole pineapple.

Yesterday we were welcomed lavishly at the airport with ukulele music and dark delightful girls, giggling in grass skirts. We arrived here at the hotel covered in fragrant garlands of flowers, and considerable relief at there being no concert to play, because the concert that was scheduled for last night was cancelled and paid for by Jack Maxwell who thought the orchestra would benefit from a free day at this stage in the tour. The American part, now complete, began in Washington, then New York, Chicago, Boston Philadelphia, Los Angeles and San Francisco.

Tomorrow we will leave for Sydney, then Melbourne, before Japan, Hong Kong, Singapore, Bangkok, Kuala Lumpur, and home via Bahrain.

Tony Chidell and I share a room from time to time, and here in the Hawaiian village we have a chalet with flowers everywhere and every imaginable luxury, including a split-level bathroom with a sunken bath. There's a swimming pool too with a cocktail bar in the middle and underwater stools you swim out to. Tony likes the good life as much as I do.

LETTERS, LINES AND SPACES

In Washington on the first day, in the sort of calm before the storm, we sent down for a breakfast of eggs Benedict and toast, which we ate in bed while watching the Woody Woodpecker show.

Completing the U.S. part really was a milestone. On the last day in San Francisco Jim Brown and I had a day out together. We ate a gigantic lobster at Fisherman's Wharf and took a boat trip to Alcatraz Island. sending a picture postcard of it, inscribed "wish you were here", to Sidney Sax who still owes us money.

As for the music, Mahler 5 still predominates the programming, with Mahler 1 providing the light relief on selected nights.

Like you, I love Mahler when he is lyrical but there's a brutality and masochism in the music that always wears me down, I suppose it's like touring in that way that sitting by the soothing sea comes between the clangour of airports, tannoys and screaming jet engines.

The Chicago concert frightened me a bit I will admit. Quite a few of the Chicago Symphony players were there and it was a difficult programme that came from Abbado and his wanting to show us off to his Chicago audience I suspect, but it went very well all the same, and afterwards, Dale Clevenger, the first horn player in the symphony orchestra took a few of us out to supper at his favourite Italian restaurant, a lovely, relaxing place, hung with tiffany lamps and buzzing with after-concert conversation. I got to bed at two a.m., full of seafood linguine and Frascati, wondering whether Bartok's Miraculous Mandarin had ever been played as an encore before.

I'm told that the printed onslaught on the L.S.O. from Private Eye continues in "Lunchtime O'Boulez". We can't get it here I'm pleased to say but reports come by

LETTERS, LINES AND SPACES

telephone from London telling me that I haven't been mentioned yet and I'm grateful for that.

You and I haven't seen each other since the strike. That's three years ago, incredible though it may seem. I hope everyone is well and happy and that the Sinfonia is thriving. Have you heard from David Hasslam or Chris Gough? You COULD write to me if you've a mind to. I'll be at the Hilton in Bangkok in about a fortnight. Have you ever tried to write a letter? It's a simple thing anyone can do. If you want to be a gent's outfitter just refer to trousers in the singular. If you want to be a conductor don't put your arms in the sleeves of your jacket. Just put pen to paper. See what happens.

Pat Vermont, flamboyant and camper than ever, regards this tour as a major upheaval of great magnitude, like a world war.
"When all this is over", he said before the Boston concert.
"I'm going back to Jamaica to live with my auntie! I simply can't stand to see another hotel. Air conditioning makes me sneeze all the time. The staff is insufferably rude...The bed-linen is filthy, the food is inedible and the coffee is poison."

Pat still entertains us all nightly like that fading old actress throwing kisses to everyone, but no one in particular because there is no one, except his Jamaican auntie he told me. We are his only family now. The nightly theatre in camera of the orchestral bandroom is only for we privileged ones. What a wonderful life we have and I wish you were here. Newcastle could never be like this.

It would be a real thrill to get a letter from you, with Novocastrian family and Sinfonia news. I'm going to hit Honolulu now where we've been advised to go out only in groups. How exciting!!

Joy and happiness to all
Drac

LETTERS, LINES AND SPACES

THE GRUELING SCHEDULES AND MONOTONY OF TOURING WITH AN ORCHESTRA CAN ALIENATE ONE FROM ONES OWN FEELINGS, AND THE BEST INTENTIONS OF EVEN THE GREATEST COMPOSERS.

Darling

We are hardly started with this tour, but my mind and body are complaining to me, and the nightly Mahler doesn't help me a bit. In everyday life I do all I can to avoid the company of negative and self-pitying people, and I have never wanted to be a witness to suffering. Whilst I play Mahler for money, and despite the mastery of the writing, I still wonder why so many want to be part of his elaborate anguish. I am sure that these are feelings one is meant to encounter at rare moments in ones life, not to be reconstituted at eight o'clock every night in a strange city.

Mozart, youthful and simple usually begins the tour programme and it's always the best part of every day. The days are spent mostly in good companionship, and exciting new places, but I do relish the time with myself when the music's over.

I imagine you are alone by now too, and the children must be asleep, but New York never sleeps, so it is said, and I seldom do when I'm here.

The clattering of delivery trucks, and wailing sirens keep me awake for half the night, but there is time to write letters, and to think of you and the children, remembering all the happiness we have when we're together.

I think about our restaurant dream, and all the time we spent talking about it. I would never have to leave you again, people would come for miles for your poached salmon and strawberry shortcake, and I could eat your cooking every day instead of hamburgers and snakes. – I could play the piano, peel potatoes, do the washing up and the fighting. -- I'll write from every city.

LETTERS, LINES AND SPACES

We were simply meant to be together.

Love forever

Drac

LETTERS, LINES AND SPACES

LSO Horns 1982 (l-r Me, Tony Chidell, Jim Brown, David Cripps (princ.))

JEFF LLOYD, A WELL-KNOWN VIOLINIST AND MUSIC ADMINISTRATOR IN SOUTH WALES, WAS LEADER OF THE NATIONAL YOUTH ORCHESTRA OF WALES DURING MY TIME THERE. KURT GOEDECKE WAS THE LSO'S TIMPANIST, AND JACK LONG WAS A VETERAN CELLIST WHO HAD PLAYED WITH JOSEPH KRIPS AND PAUL HINDEMITH. JACK RETIRED IN 1984, AFTER A CAREER IN ORCHESTRAL PLAYING, OF FIFTY YEARS.

Hotel Rossia
Moscow

November 1983

Dear Jeff

Greetings from the largest hotel in the world. They have three thousand four hundred rooms here and I'm on the fourteenth floor, which gives me a fabulous view of the Kremlin and the city. The streets have been completely cleared of snow after a storm during the night, and out in the streets, the air is so cold that it paralyzes the lungs when you breathe, but we got to the conservatory last night with plenty of time to thaw out before we played Stravinsky and Shostakovich to a huge audience, all stamping and cheering. The audience here is so warm and appreciative, you find yourself being hugged and kissed by perfect strangers at the stage door. We had no idea that we were so well known in Russia. The whole world has seen Star Wars now, and that seems to be what we're famous for here. I'm amazed !!

Rank Xerox, who are sponsoring the tour, gave us a wonderful reception after the concert. The hugging and kissing continued and the food was really delicious—real caviar, smoked salmon and ice cream with fresh fruit, which was very welcome to us, the food at the hotel being almost inedible, and the fact that there are hardly any restaurants in Moscow.

During the day, a few of us, desperate for a good meal, were escorted, by our tour guide to a restaurant, which was open for business, despite it's being in the process of re-painting and decorating. The waiter brought some very sweet, sparkling wine, that the Russians call Champagne, while Kurt Goedecke chatted in German to a man on a ladder, who was painting the wall next to our table, and Jack Long, who speaks in Cockney rhyming slang almost all the time, was trying to explain its mysteries to our young Russian tour guide, who smiled politely but obviously hadn't the faintest idea what it was about or why anyone would want to take the trouble to understand it. When we'd waited for more than an hour for the food, which was cold when it came, Jack found something in his beetroot soup that he couldn't decide was cream or emulsion paint, so none of us ate very much.

Before we left London, the trombones who had been here before, strongly advised bringing emergency provisions, so I had packed some tinned meat and fish, fruit, vacuum packed cheese and biscuits to keep me going. I hope that things might be better in St Petersburg.

LETTERS, LINES AND SPACES

It was good yesterday, even in the perishing cold, to have time to go to St Basil's cathedral to wander around Moscow, and I can assure you we weren't spied on or followed. All that is so much propaganda and nonsense I'm sure.

To kill time before the concert and to defer coming back to this bleak hotel, we wandered in the shops, and were able to buy one or two presents. Tomorrow we'll give another concert at the conservatory and immediately afterwards we'll take the night train to St Petersburg.

While I was buying the presents, I felt a sudden and powerful longing for home. I've never before felt quite like that. I'm sure it's just that we've been away so much this year, and in case you're wondering, I'm still thinking seriously of buying a little hotel or a pub in Wales, and I'll be going to Brecon and Llantrisant for some exploration, when we get back. We could meet up in Cardiff if you're around.

Life without the daily grind of hotels, airports and foreign cities is becoming more attractive to me all the time now, but the resilience and humour of musicians keeps me going. Jack said in the interval last night that his bottle of duty free "Vera Lynn", had disappeared from his room. He didn't seem to mind at all.
"They don't have much", he said.
Jack started his musical journey over forty years ago in cafes and theatre pits, and he's relished "every minute", but he's been no stranger to hardship.

I'll telephone when I'm home and my feet are warm again. It should only take a week or two.

Luv

Drac

LETTERS, LINES AND SPACES

Intermission Abbey Road

THE CITY OF LONDON CORPORATION OPENED THE BARBICAN ARTS CENTRE IN 1982, AFTER A GREAT DEAL OF PRE-PUBLICITY. THE CONCERT HALL, WHICH WAS BUILT ON A GERMAN BOMB SITE BECAME THE PERMANENT HOME OF THE LONDON SYMPHONY ORCHESTRA, WHO GAVE THE OPENING CONCERT ON THE 3RD OF MARCH OF THAT YEAR.

Dear Pat

Did you enjoy the concert? How marvellous it was to see you after all this time, and looking so well!

I wonder if you think London has changed a lot since you left, and do you go to concerts in Ireland? I haven't been to one for years, but we've have played a hell of a lot of them in the run up to the opening of the new hall. There have been a few grand dinners too, hosted by worshipful companies in the City of London, and all sorts of pre – events. At one of these we played some brass quintets at a party in the roof garden while a lot of rich and famous people were drinking champagne.

LETTERS, LINES AND SPACES

When we'd been playing for what seemed like hours, and watching enviously while the elegant assemblage stuffed themselves with smoked salmon and fine wine, Ted Heath and David Jacobs suddenly appeared at the bandstand!

"Sounds awfully good", Heath said through his trademark grin.

"It'd sound even better if we 'ad a f***ing drink" said Maurice Murphy, which shocked one or two innocent bystanders. People weren't aware of course, that Maurice and Heath had been well acquainted for years, and understood one another perfectly, so we started the next number, which was a particularly awful arrangement of William Tell. When we got to the galop, I saw from the corner of my eye, the crowd of people smiling, applauding, and making way for the ex Prime minister who was striding towards us, still grinning, and carrying a tray with three bottles of Cordon Rouge, followed closely by David Jacobs with five glasses!

We've had a lot of fun recently, and you arrived at the funniest part. The concert you came to was just great, maybe even the best one of all!

Someone told me you would be there, and eventually, I spotted you in the audience, laughing helplessly at George Burns. He really enjoyed himself too, cracking jokes backstage with the brass, in a backstage tableau that should have been recorded for posterity. Tony Bennett didn't want to rehearse much, which annoyed the television people. David Frost would have run the whole thing a dozen times if he'd been allowed to, and Harry Rabinovitz kept it all together, relishing all the theatrical mayhem and bonhomie. It was the perfect finishing touch, to see you sitting there splitting your sides.

On the following evening, at the real opening concert, I felt a little disappointed that the "fun" part of the week was at an end, and I fully expected that the presence of our gracious Queen, the Lord Mayor of London, a good number of noble Lords and Ladies, and a "live" television relay, might bring a stiff reminder of the importance of the occasion and some propriety to the proceedings. However, Tony Chidell was born without any trace of deferential or ceremonial genes, and could be heard whispering at convenient moments, that "Die Meistersinger" was "Hitler's favourite piece", and that its inclusion in the programme was probably in honour and gratitude for his "having cleared the site!"

My priorities, and the tradition and importance of humour were restored, and we had a lovely evening in our new home. It was wonderful to see you again. It's such a pity everyone had to rush off afterwards to somewhere else. When was it ever any different for us?

Yours Ever

Drac

LETTERS, LINES AND SPACES

With Jack Brymer in Sibelius's Garden at Jarvenpaa

IN 1983 THE LSO RECORDED THE SOUNDTRACK FOR THE "RETURN OF THE JEDI" WHICH WAS THE THIRD OF THE STAR WARS FILMS TO BE MADE.

Dear Martin,

I passed through Newcastle on the train last month while listening to Radio 3. Naturally, I was wondering how you were, when quite coincidentally, a broadcast from Newcastle started, just as the train pulled out of the station, - E.J. Moeran's music it was, from the Sinfonia centre. Despite the inadequacy of my little Walkman, headphones, and the noise of the train, I really enjoyed it, and the horns sounded great! I always admired his music, It's just beautiful, and I've never played a note of it in all these years.!

I was travelling up north on a "Shell-LSO" concert tour, and as part of our family plan to relocate and recalibrate ourselves, I broke off to view a couple of hotels that were for sale, and once or twice, I thought we might get to be neighbours again but I wasn't moved to make any decisions by what I saw.

LETTERS, LINES AND SPACES

This is all proving to be more difficult than I imagined it would be, because a lot of the businesses are for sale on account of trading difficulties, and touring the north of England I've been shocked at the state of the country and the boarded-up shops and industrial wreckage. It's obvious to me now that we haven't felt the impact of the downturn so much in London, even though the LSO did hit another financial crisis, shortly after we opened the Barbican hall and called on Raymond Gubbay to help out.

Anyhow, we're still in business and last week we recorded the sound track for "Return of the Jedi", but we had to go to Abbey Road to do it, Denham having being finally closed.

I will miss going there. What a film history it had! A draughty old aircraft hangar, where you could break your neck in the dark with all those cables lying about, and Oliver, Fiddler on the roof, Dracula, Star Wars, Superman, Indiana Jones, all recorded there. What an inventory! Not to mention the dramas that were enacted off the screen.

Getting the sack from "Battle of Britain" along with Walton and Malcolm Arnold was one such, followed by Gilbey's gin and bitter recrimination at the village pub.

"The Return of the Jedi" was done in the usual congenial atmosphere, and all great fun. Darth Vader was Wagnerially incinerated at the end, accompanied by a horn solo from yours truly, and the great delight of Pat Vermont who always refers to him as "that horrid asthmatic man!"

"Oh mercy! Why does the vilest person in the universe have to be black?" he has been pleading since 1977.

He told me discreetly, to avoid offending the delicate sensibilities of the trombones, that he always dreaded Darth's appearance on the screen because it involved more loud trombone music. He's wearied by sitting in front of them for thirty years I think, but his going back to Jamaica to live with his auntie is scheduled definitely for next year, he says.

It did seem strange doing a film session in that studio. I can only associate it with those formal introductions, foreign accents and photographers from the "Gramophone", but we're still laughing here as you can tell.

I hope you still do lots of laughing in the Sinfonia. Give my love to the family. I wonder, do the children have a Geordie accent? Ours are learning "Saaarf" London.

Luv Drac

LETTERS, LINES AND SPACES

"When you arrive on market day, a choir will be forming in a corner of the public bar"

WE BOUGHT THE BULL'S HEAD HOTEL IN BRECON IN 1984, FOR A DIFFERENT WAY OF LIFE AWAY FROM LONDON. IN WALES YOU ARE NEVER FAR AWAY FROM MUSIC.

Mr. Pat O'Brian

Theo Connelly Fine Instruments

DUBLIN

The Bull's Head Hotel

The Struet

Brecon

Powys

Wales

23rd January 1985

Dear Pat

At last I find myself alone in the saloon bar of the Bull's Head, except for the spirits of old soldiers and ancient sons of the soil. They like to see the brass gleaming and the mirrors sparkling, and they always leave the place exactly as they find it, for the reappearance of the public at six o'clock.

LETTERS, LINES AND SPACES

How exciting it was this morning to find your letter among the pile of bills and brewery boredom. I have your room all ready for your visit. It sits at the very top of the house, overlooking the cathedral grounds and the river Honddu where she quickens with excitement, and tumbles into the Usk for the journey down to Newport. I know you will feel at perfect ease in The Bull's Head.

It stands solid and symmetrically Georgian, just above the Watergate, and when you arrive on market day, a choir will be forming in a corner of the public bar and the till will be full of grubby old banknotes and straw.

I often settle at the piano on market days and I've been wondering if you would bring a fiddle with you. We could give them some Mozart, or even a bit of old Ireland. Everyone loves music here and there is a lot of musical activity too, with the choir and the Gwent chamber orchestra that gives concerts regularly in the cathedral. And there's the local male voice choir, and the jazz festival that takes place every summer. This old Georgian town will be home from home for you, I know you will have a great time.

Our customers delight the summer visitors with their diversity. The public bar is always buzzing with squaddies, farm boys and Ghurkha soldiers, while the officers, lawyers, and landowners have their lunch in the back bar. My lawyer, John Llewelyn, eats lunch here regularly, of dressed crab or partridge, washed down with Muscadet or Puligny Montrachet to fortify his eighteen stone frame for the battles, over land registry and fishing rights that dominate proceedings in the Powys county court.

He completes the 'Times' crossword every day, entirely in his head, during the walk to the "Bull's Head", from his office in the town.
There's an old circuit judge too, who comes fortnightly to Brecon for bassoon lessons. On one foot, he wears an English handmade shoe and on the other, a carpet slipper to soften the pain of his gout. Two or three times a year a bearded banana boat captain,

LETTERS, LINES AND SPACES

who sails between Swansea and St.Kitts comes home from the sea and I sell him navy rum -- and there are several ex paratroopers and SAS men, who live in Brecon when they're not body guarding Saudi dignitaries. Erstwhile Welsh rugby heroes come to sell me beer and sportswear, and on special days, a good many players from the B.B.C. National Orchestra of Wales drop in for their lunch on the way to Bangor or Aberystwyth.

Barry Booth and Rolf Harris, who were touring Wales, called to see me the other week. Within ten minutes of arriving Barry had discovered my piano in the back bar, and Rolf was into one of his many bawdy songs for the entertainment of our three mid-morning customers. There were two farmers and sheepdogs in the bar and an old tired looking private dick who had been hanging around for a few days, looking for somebody. Tom Jenkins Bronllys, who had never seen a celebrity before, in the flesh, observed that Rolf looked just like "that bloke off the tele", although he couldn't be sure. I accused him of being drunk, and threatened to curtail his cider ration.

Tom's morning cider and whisky cocktail makes him uncertain of almost everything that happens after eleven o'clock.

Life is grand here. Karin loves it too, and her cooking is already locally famous, but I do fear that our idyllic peace may be soon coming to an end, the manager of the B.B.C. Welsh having persuaded me to sign a contract for a broadcast with them, to take place in October, which will at least allow me plenty of time to practice.

I am looking forward to seeing you again, more than you can imagine and my father is delighted too, having heard so much about you. He's been living above ground now for ten years or so and enjoys his life immensely; especially market day at the "Bull's head" spent jawing with the farmers.

Til the 17th

LETTERS, LINES AND SPACES

Drac

P.S. We have Guinness and old Jameson's whiskey.

LETTERS, LINES AND SPACES

THE BRECON BY-ELECTION WAS AN EVENT THAT WAS OF GREAT ELECTORAL IMPORTANCE IN A BRITAIN THAT WAS SUFFERING FROM HIGH UNEMPLOYMENT AND THE DESTRUCTION OF ITS MINING INDUSTRY AS THE RESULT OF GOVERNMENT POLICIES AND A MINERS' STRIKE THAT LASTED MORE THAN A YEAR.

The Bull's Head Hotel
Brecon
Powys
Wales

December 1987

Dear Bob

The jazz festival is done for another year. Brecon has gone back to bed, and the farmers and sheepdogs have restored pastoral calm and melodious Welsh language to the public bar. Now that things are quieter, I can walk by the river in the afternoons, and talk to the locals without the obfuscations of alcohol and a bar between us.

In July the by-election in Brecon was front-page news, and it brought a lot of media people here. Kinnock came with a lot of pre-publicity, to try to bolster the Labour vote, and the security for his visit was formidable. He wrote to say that he would be coming to Brecon, and would "drop in" but I'd no idea how much palaver there would be beforehand.

On the evening he arrived, to make his "informal" visit to the "Bull's Head" the telephone rang in the bar, and to my surprise, a special branch person, after interrogating me thoroughly with regard to my identity, told me that the ". ...Leader of the opposition would be arriving in thirteen minutes".

At exactly the appointed time two men with trench coats, walkie-talkies and everything came in to the bar and asked me if we were ready to "receive the leader of Her

LETTERS, LINES AND SPACES

Majesty's Opposition". The sound of the police radios' nasal chattering in the street outside, and the blue lights flashing made one or two of our public bar customers a bit nervous I think!!

Anyway, he finally arrived with some more official looking people and John Cole, the BBC's chief political guy. Neil looks so comfortable now with all those trappings of power. It does me good to see it. I hope he can change things. When we were in the Glamorgan Youth, I remember he was almost always surrounded by people, laughing and enjoying themselves. He's a born leader, but he loves people –and it shows!

We have some intriguing customers. There's an old guy who was at one time the getaway driver, for a well-known firm of bank robbers. Having been paid handsomely by his old firm for confessing to some crime of which he was entirely innocent, he spent part of his life in jail, thus enabling his former employers to continue their illegal activities unhindered. He used the considerable sum of money he received, for this inconvenience, to pay for his son to go to law school, and now, in his old age, he likes nothing better than to come to the Bull's Head, drink Guinness, and discuss legal and criminal matters with the old circuit judge from Machynlleth, who relishes the company of the criminal classes

" Wonderful people! -- Our bread and butter", he calls them.

There's an old colonel too, who comes in mostly in the mornings, shrouded in pipe smoke. He's an ex-MI6, agent, so the military contingent tells me.

And there's a furtive archaeologist that the locals call "Eric the Relic". The rest are farmers, colliers, soldiers, teachers, cathedral choristers, lawyers, landowners, clergymen, musicians, scoundrels, and wasters. Neil was at ease with everybody.

LETTERS, LINES AND SPACES

Things have been very tough here for most people in recent years and the year long miners' strike has been almost the last straw, so business hasn't been very profitable, and I've been spending a lot of time in Cardiff, playing at the BBC. But we've recently had a very good offer for the freehold of the Bull's and I've been offered some work teaching and playing in Scotland, so after a lot of discussion we've decided to sell. We're both exhausted with eighteen-hour days and no holidays, but working for a living has been a new experience for me, and it tells me what a real privilege it is to be able to make a living from music. So we're off once more. Karin will be happy to be in Edinburgh again. What a shame you haven't been able to visit us. How is the club? I haven't been to Cardiff for a while I'm sorry to say.

Come and see us before we go! We'll have a farewell jazz night.

Yours ever

Terry J

LETTERS, LINES AND SPACES

86 Tramway
Hirwaun

30th October 1989

Dear Martin

Father died in a hospital in Merthyr a few days ago from lung cancer. I knew that he had not been well, but mother had been saying continually, that it was nothing at all serious, so it came as a huge shock to be told in a telephone call from Avril Weston, a neighbour and friend of the family, that he had died. The lady was so obviously distressed and confused by everything that had happened, and very surprised at how ill equipped Mother had been to deal with something like this. She had obviously been unable to cope with it all, and for some reason, had tried to keep his illness a secret from everyone. In despair finally, it seems she turned to Avril for help. In her panic and confusion, mother wasn't even able to speak to me directly, so she asked Avril to do it. She may have found it difficult to admit, even to herself, how serious his illness was.

It was a huge shock to get the telephone call, but when I had composed myself I couldn't really be angry with Mother. She never was very robust mentally, as you will remember. She found it difficult to cope with even the slightest difficulty in her life, and relied on my father for everything. So this, of all things must have seemed insurmountable to her. I did feel for Avril though, and for her predicament. I hadn't spoken to her for many years, so she had to re-introduce herself before telling me very painfully what the call was about.

I don't know how I feel now, apart from the worry of what will happen to Mother. She won't come to live with us in Scotland that much is certain. We've argued over it so many times in recent years. I really don't know how she will deal with life, living alone, and without him. Having been married to her for fifty years, he understood, better even than the doctors, what was wrong with her. He accepted her illness completely, even though it caused her to be very abusive to him at times you know, which is the more remarkable considering the other difficulties he experienced in his life.

I tell you all this, because to you and many others that knew him, he appeared to be so introverted and certainly never complained about anything, and not many people knew much about him.

When he was just fourteen, he lost his own father and went to work at Tower colliery to support his mother and his two younger brothers. He was in the strike in 1926 and three explosions in that pit before the war came in 1939 and he joined the RAF as a dispatch rider, stationed in London through all the blitz and the doodlebugs, and after they had a child stillborn in 1942, I was born in Paddington in 1944, and we went back to Wales when the war ended.

His mother had worked for most of her life, as a farm girl in Penderyn, having been adopted from the orphanage by the farmer, as was often the practice in those days. The farmers avoided paying wages that way, exchanging only food and lodgings for labour. She could not read or write, and father told me that she struggled quite a bit with English, Welsh being her first language. My grandfather who also could neither read nor write, was a Cornish builder who came to Wales to build miners cottages in 1907. When he died suddenly, Father was forced to leave school to go into the mines, and I always believed he wanted, more than anything for me to go to grammar school and further education. I'm so grateful to them you know, for all those music lessons and youth orchestra courses that must have cost them so much of their hard earned money. This is all so painful to me now, remembering how they never had any money for anything, never having had a chance to get an education for themselves.

I must stop now. My head is spinning. I just can't imagine what will happen to Mother, and I will have to go back to Scotland at some point. She didn't go to the funeral. This

LETTERS, LINES AND SPACES

Welsh all male funeral custom is something I'll never understand. She just sits for hours now in her chair without speaking to anyone.

Yours ever

Drac

LETTERS, LINES AND SPACES

12 Clifton Terrace
Edinburgh

10th April 1993

Dear Pat

Your letters always cheer me and make me laugh. I never imagined that it could be so much fun, working in a violin saleroom.

Karin and I intend to come to Dublin for a weekend some time soon, She would like to buy some Irish linen and Waterford crystal to bring " some lovely Ireland " into the house, and I want to wander round the writers' museum and come and see you. Could we meet? It's been such a long time it seems since our weekend at the Bull's Head, swimming in that black beer and Irish music. I wonder if the weekends are a busy time for you. Will you write and tell me if it's all right? We'll most likely be there on the last weekend in June when the BBC orchestra is on holiday, which I'm looking forward to immensely.

Orchestras are nothing like what they used to be you know. Life at the BBC is just a round of mediocre performances, with the odd flash of brilliance that reminds you of why you took up music in the first place. But the most part, which I can't get used to at all, seems to be one great fuss about third rate contemporary music, silly dress codes, personality clashes, and health and safety. I don't think you would enjoy yourself much now. No one argues with conductors any more. It's strictly forbidden, though nothing's changed much of course, and many of them still don't have the faintest idea what they're meant to be doing. All that is all very well, but it's very difficult to have humour with a lot of what we used to think of as badinage having been reclassified as "harassment" and it's humour that has always kept me going in orchestral life. I miss it a lot.

LETTERS, LINES AND SPACES

This will interest you! Do you remember Horace Naismith and that beautiful Guardagnini he had? Well that violin had quite a history. I learned recently that it survived miraculously, when the Queen's Hall burned down in 1941. The hall got a direct hit from an incendiary bomb at about eleven o'clock at night. Horace was in the orchestra there as you know, and the violin, which he had left in the bandroom overnight, came floating out like Noah's Ark, on the flood from the fire hoses, only because it was in a flimsy old ply- wood box that he'd knocked up for it, Horace having sold its heavy and very expensive cedar wood velvet lined case to someone in the orchestra for money to put on a horse that was running at Ascot. Bill Naughtie told me all this in a letter, when Horace had died recently, in very reduced circumstances it seems.

Bill said in his letter, that the Guardagnini had also been sold finally, for a great deal of money, although he couldn't say to whom. Horace was quite a man wasn't he? Imagine leaving an instrument like that in the band room in the middle of the Blitz! No wonder so many people wondered how he had acquired it in the first place?

But he was a charming English gentleman, typical of those people in the Royal Philharmonic in the seventies. When I started to play first horn there, I remember getting a particularly severe public roasting one morning, from a very rude and excitable French conductor, and after the rehearsal, when I was seething in the spit and sawdust of "Dirty Dick's", next door, Horace appeared in his perfectly tailored sports jacket, drink in hand. "I do like champagne in the mornin's", he said, smacking his lips. "Don't take it personally old boy", he said. "He's not listenin' to YOU, you know ---- Has his own ideas. Long plane journeys --- Too much time to think. --- You'll learn!! -- Just play the notes. Don't give 'em any music. That's a mistake. I'm sure some actually find it offensive --- They think that's their department you see. Music's too good for orchestral players you know ---. Tommy Beecham was different".

LETTERS, LINES AND SPACES

I learned such a lot there from people like him. He always said that all that recording was a bad idea, and that it would all end in tears one day, and he was certainly right about that.

I well remember you warning me, tactfully, on one of my first tours, about Horace and his winning, or should I say beguiling, ways, particularly with regard to borrowing money. I'm sure he still owes me ten dollars! He's welcome to it. It was worth it for the wise words.

I'm hugely looking forward to coming to Dublin for a few days. Though I enjoy myself immensely here in Edinburgh, visiting the galleries and exploring the city.

When I'm not doing that I drive around Scotland doing concerts with the BBC Scottish and the Scottish ballet company, from Dumfries up to Orkney. Scotland is breathtakingly beautiful and Karin is so happy to be back at last.

I'll be going to Wales tomorrow to see my mother, who is in hospital. She was admitted on Friday, but didn't let me know. When she hadn't answered her telephone for two days, I got a little anxious and called her neighbour, who told me where she was. I've become used to her eccentricities over many years, but things have certainly become more difficult and worrying since Father died.

How is your mother? I wonder if she would remember me. If she does please give her my best regards, I hope she still sings. I will never forget her beautiful voice, and all those Irish songs I had never heard before. Imagine yourself as a babe in arms, and that music being the first you had ever heard in this world!!! It's not a bit surprising that contemporary music irritates you so much. The BBC would drive you mad in a week I'm sure.

Dreaming of Dublin!!!

LETTERS, LINES AND SPACES

Luv ever

Drac

PS   Some time in the seventies it was -- after you had left London – Horace ran in to a Lord someone or other that he'd been at Eton with. Well - evidently they got a bit pissed in the Salisbury Arms in St Martin's Lane, and the pubs closed at three in the afternoon in those days, so the noble Lord invited Horace back to the Palace of Westminster in order to continue their congenial reunion, where no such prohibitions applied. Lord X's sole means of transport was a push bike that he'd left outside the pub, so Horace (you'll remember he was quite a small man) got on the cross bar, and they set off!! The story goes that they freewheeled, somewhat erratically down St. Martin's Lane and Trafalgar Square, as far as Horse Guards before being stopped by a policeman and charged with something – I'm not sure what!

I must go K is calling me for Friday fish.

LETTERS, LINES AND SPACES

12 Clifton Terrace
Edinburgh

25th April 1993

Dear Martin

Mother died, in peace at last, in Mountain Ash a few days ago, shortly after I had reluctantly left the hospital to come back to Scotland. The staff there had been so kind and helpful to me, and one of the doctors, who knew her well, told me that she had in fact been quite close to death on the last occasion they had taken her to that hospital. That had happened more than a year ago without my knowledge, and they told me that they had been surprised when she had survived the journey. So he urged me, gently and calmly, to attend to the things I had to do, and to trust him, and the staff to look after her.

I remember starting for Edinburgh, feeling a little more comfortable about it all, and I slept for a while on the train, but finally as I put the key into the lock at Clifton Terrace, I could hear the telephone ringing from inside the flat and I knew immediately that it was all over. The doctor I had spoken to in Wales told me that Mother had died very peacefully, an hour or so after I had left the hospital. The first thing I felt was relief, really because she had been so ill for so many years, not just with her many physical ailments, but her mental state was something no one was able to help her with, as you know. When I was a boy and she was young, there were lots of happy times, and I remember her smile and her optimism. Later on I believe she began to suffer from a fear of people that her disordered mind could only express in the form of anger and contempt. When I left the valleys to study music in London it was a tragedy for her, and she spoke about the loss of her first child as she often did when she was in her lowest spirits.

LETTERS, LINES AND SPACES

I will try to remember her laughing, and warm like the little kitchen we had at the house in Baptist place. There are very few people to whom I would entrust such feelings. You and I have been such great friends for such a long time. You mustn't mind. I feel as if I have lost my bearings.

Relief sorrow and guilt make such a confusing and debilitating mixture, but I must get on. Sally and Dylan are just setting out in life and Karin is at home at last, here in Edinburgh where she was born. I love to see her so happy –

> "For each age is a dream that is dying,
> Or one that is coming to birth"

Yours ever

Drac

LETTERS, LINES AND SPACES

MY FRIEND JOHN GREEN, THE WELSH NOVELIST, PLAYWRIGHT, AND AUTHOR OF "REUNION", AND "THE STONE FRIGATE", WAS A REGULAR CUSTOMER AT THE BULL'S HEAD. HE ENCOURAGED ME, DURING OUR YEARS THERE, TO PREPARE THESE LETTERS FOR PUBLICATION.

Mr John Green
50 Camden Road
BRECON
Powys

Kirkwall Hotel
Orkney

Dear John

I'm in my hotel room at last, after a tedious journey from Amsterdam that ended with a bone-jarring flight from Aberdeen in a tiny aeroplane, and a half hour squashed with four others into a twenty five year old Austin Maxi, which represents, I think, a half of the Kirkwall taxi fleet. The sky is still light, despite the lateness of the hour, which is approaching ten thirty, and light evenings somehow depress my spirits, for reasons that I can't explain, but I can summon gratitude enough to thank God for sparing me the horrors of having to play any of Peter Maxwell Davies' music, which although some was included in the programme for tonight, included no horns in the score.

Is Brecon full with summer tourists? I hope the jazz festival rang all the bells of the tills of the town for three days, flooding the streets and pubs with devil's music. How I love devil's music!!

In Amsterdam we played Tchaikovsky and Beethoven and people sat, as they always do, in silence and reverence, waiting for the compulsory show of appreciation, which must be a huge relief for many. I know it is for me. The thought of another suffering in silence of Beethoven's pastoral symphony provokes the same feelings in me, as does this vase of nearly dead flowers on the table in this dismal room, marooned as I am with

LETTERS, LINES AND SPACES

Maxwell - bloody - Davies on this island that can't decide whether it's night or day. But tomorrow in the morning, we will give a concert of mostly new music, for the children who come by hundreds, in boats from all the neighbouring islands and clap and cheer whenever they feel like it, and I'll be out of here in a couple of days, headed for London and the Proms, that are always a joy. I wonder what music in Britain could do without them. The BBC orchestras could not survive certainly.

The autumn concert season in Scotland will start soon enough after that, and there will be howling winds and snow on the pass at Drumochter and the audiences will arrive at Inverness, capped and mufflered and despite it all. But before the snow falls I'll come to see you at Brecon and we can spend a market day together, leaning on the bar with the farmers and Ghurkas. I'll send you a postcard from lascivious London where I know so many people that I can't look them all up in three days so I'll wriggle in and out like a jellied eel.

Good luck John

Yours as ever

Terry

LETTERS, LINES AND SPACES

HAVING ASSUMED THAT MY TOURING DAYS WERE OVER, I WAS INVITED BY THE BBC SCOTTISH SYMPHONY ORCHESTRA TO TOUR THE USA, LATVIA, ESTONIA, CHINA AND SOUTH AMERICA

Mr.John Green   Shangri-la Hotel
50 Camden Road   Guangzhou
BRECON
Powys

October 2000

Dear John

The tour is nearly done and my diabetes has survived a week in China and the severe test of a diet of eels, snakes, prawns and rice so I'm glad to say that tomorrow we'll go to Taiwan for one more concert before going home. The atmosphere in the streets of Guangzhou feels quite threatening, and professional ladies and drug dealers surround the hotel after dark, so after the concert I decided to stay out of harms way in my room and write some letters and Christmas cards.

I hear Christmas music everywhere here, in restaurants and lifts and the presents of silk and jade I have bought to take back are lying in my hotel room gift - wrapped for Christmas and make me feel homesick when I see them. How are things in Brecon? Will the family be visiting you at Christmas? I imagine Brecon will be glowing with lanterns and log fires by now. I want to get home to the family. Our journey from London seemed interminable, and we had to wait more than three hours in the bedlam of Hong Kong airport for our connection to Shanghai but it was all worthwhile, because it has been a remarkable experience. During the last hour of the flight I think I was the only person apart from the cabin crew who was still awake, after a great deal of complimentary wine and brandy from the airline had been served with dinner and, as you know I haven't had an alcoholic drink for a good while. I enjoyed the best of clear-headedness and watched the sun rising as, everybody was sleeping, approaching Shanghai, when the party in the cabin was over and there was only the whine of the engines. The dawn appeared as a faint purple line along the horizon and soon, I could see outlines of the hills and valleys below us stretching away from the wing of the plane for miles with no trace of civilization. Then some activity began in the cabin with gentle waking, murmuring, breakfast and hot coffee.

The grand new airport at Shanghai was all but deserted when we arrived, and there were very few cars on the city streets. I don't know how many tours I've been on over all these years, and when we owned the Bull's Head, I told myself I didn't miss travelling, but I still find different countries excite me, I enjoyed exploring the city when we didn't have to play on the first day and we could visit the Yuyuan garden, the city temple and the reclining Buddha.

Near the hotel, there's a restaurant that serves every kind of fish and shellfish, all kept in tanks and aquariums that decorate the walls, and so I went there with the trombones, in search of eels. My twenty years, living in London has given me a real taste for them, and I'm always surprised that so many people find the thought of eating them disgusting. The Chinese chef came to our table, and showed us the wriggling eels before chopping them alive and throwing them into a flaming wok, with pungent garlic and black bean sauce. I could feel the effects of homesickness and the long journey ebbing away and China began to beguile me at last. Later I slept like Methuselah and the next day's concert was a real joy. The audience were wild about it, especially the Scottish eightsome reel we saved as an encore.

Good luck John and the merriest Christmas ever.

Terry

LETTERS, LINES AND SPACES

DAVID HUGHES WAS A MUSIC ADMINISTRATOR IN SOUTH WALES AND CONDUCTOR OF THE "THREE COUNTIES" YOUTH ORCHESTRA.

The Murrays
Edinburgh
EH17 8UN

8th August 2006

Dear Dave

It was wonderful to see you again after all these years. I always look forward to the "Proms" but your message to say that you were coming to the concert suddenly made it a very special event. I'm delighted that you enjoyed it so much. The B.B.C. Scottish is fully recovered now, as you can hear, a full quarter of a century after the strike. The Strauss was particularly good I thought.

When I left you on Friday, on that soft summer evening, I walked back to the hotel remembering our youth orchestra days together and our many old pals. It always seemed to be summer then, and one of the first things I thought of was the beauty of North Wales that was completely new to me. As you know, I grew up in the coal-blackness of the mining valleys, and it wasn't until I got into the youth orchestra that I had travelled beyond the Brecon beacons. Music suddenly set me free in the world.

I so much admire what you do for the youth orchestra now and a lot of the young people stand to gain so much from it, and I feel honoured that you want to perform my music in your January concert next year. I expect it to be a great event and a lovely reunion.

My piece "I'r Wyddel" (For an Irishman) is dedicated to Willie Lang who is one of my great heroes of music. He came from real working class roots, being a stonemason and solo cornet with Black Dyke band. He was an inspiration to everyone.

LETTERS, LINES AND SPACES

Over the credits on the film "The Man Who Would Be King", you can hear a solo cornet playing "A Minstrel Boy to the War Has Gone". You'll agree if you've heard it that it is an uniquely beautiful sound. I was at Denham when Willie recorded it with Maurice Jarre. It was that session I think that first got me thinking about the Irish and their music. The best Irish musicians I know live without many of our modern neuroses. There is no fear of anonymity or of failure for them you know, only music and gratitude. Willie's like that in his Irishness. He is the perfect hero for our children. Thanks to you and all your efforts we can give them a special event to remember.

I hope I can get Neil Kinnock to preside over the evening. It's exciting!!

Kind Regards

Terry J

PS   What a pleasure to meet your family. They live and breathe music too. It links us all together doesn't it?

LETTERS, LINES AND SPACES

Mr. Karl Jenkins

Hotel Intercontinental
Sao Paulo
Brazil

June 2007

Dear Karl

Sao Paulo is melting. The temperature is returned to the high eighties after a ferocious thunderstorm that exploded during the night after our concert, leaving the city with some cool air to breathe. My very large and luxurious hotel room has air-conditioning, grand leather furniture and lots of writing paper, so here is a letter to thank you for that marvellous concert in Glasgow. Thanks for "The Armed Man" ...Thank you for not "breaking the bondage of tonality" or "flying in the face of conventional formal concepts". To me you are a real and relevant composer, who stands, apart from the crowd of contemporary intellectuals, and their once only, hall-emptying performances, that drive orchestral players to despair and concertgoers back home to their stereo systems" Praise the Lord we are a musical nation". So say I. Although our nation is admired by no means everyone.

An hour ago I was in the hotel restaurant, alone with my two-day old "Times" crossword, and I couldn't help overhearing some post concert discourse from the only other occupied table. The BBC producer for the tour, having been robbed at gunpoint along with the sound crew, a couple of days ago in Rio, was describing the incident, probably for the hundredth time, whilst upbraiding one of the engineers, (a Welshman from Swansea, who had by this time retired to his bed) for his general demeanour, tone of voice, body language, and overall response, when faced with the prospect of a violent death in the car park of the Hotel Gloria, which apparently had risked enraging the gunman to some point beyond his normal rage level and the consequent massacre of the entire party. Cowardice, lack of negotiating skills and, inadequacy in Spanish (according to the semi drunken ranting of this producer) were shortcomings in the absent and unfortunate fellow, which were entirely attributable to his nationality. The contemptuous and monotonous monologue continued for some time, extending eventually to the entire population of Wales and most of Patagonia before I revealed myself and my annoyance. Then came a grovelling, garment rending apology, which was almost, more, embarrassing to listen to than the original offence.

Making my way to the lift I heard him say that he'd "had no idea" that I was there and then something about my spitefulness in not having shown myself sooner, thereby affirming his life long belief in the duplicity, and inherent malice of the Welsh beyond any doubt whatever.

However uncomfortable I may have felt with my supper, it isn't racism or the Times crossword that keeps me awake. I have suffered badly with the time-changes on this trip and I find myself half asleep on the platform in front of two thousand people and then, wide-awake, I sit up writing or reading for half the night.

Sao Paulo is a hell of a violent place. There was a gun battle outside the hotel shortly after we arrived and there were police cars everywhere, blood on the pavement and helicopters above. The whole thing was shown on the television news, which we watched in the bar of the hotel. The streets even in daylight are unsafe. The poverty is heartbreaking, and there is no relief whatever for the mentally ill. In Rio de Janeiro, I saw a man lying in a doorway on a filthy blanket screaming and crying and tearing at his hair, while across the street the grand houses of the rich stand towering behind electric security fences.

One of my mother's five sisters suffered with severe mental illness, and the children in the village tormented her whenever she ventured out, and my mother was not stable mentally either as I think you know.

LETTERS, LINES AND SPACES

I can remember the doctor coming to the house in the middle of the night more than once, when I was a small boy, and being made to stay in my room until he had gone. In a little miner's cottage you could hear perfectly from upstairs, every word that was being said through the rest of the house. I only remember mother shouting a lot and pleading to be left alone.

Perhaps I have an affinity with such people. I certainly formed a great friendship with Stefan Schwartz whom almost everyone in the Royal Philharmonic considered to be mad. I got along famously with him and we ate together often in the days when I smoked sixty cigarettes every day and ate very little, Stefan would eat every morsel of food that I left on my plate. Eating every scrap of waste food, even from pavements or dustbins was an obsession he had suffered, after surviving starvation in the camp at Auschwitz and I soon became accustomed to it, and was not in the least offended or disgusted as some other people were.

Stefan was gifted with the famous Jewish sense of humour and an acute sense of the ridiculous. He kept an ancient piece of paper in his wallet, which was a certificate, from one of the many institutions that had treated him in the years after the war, to say that having received appropriate treatment for his condition he was declared to be entirely sane. His response to insinuations or comments on his sanity thereafter was to brandish this document, declaring that he was the only person in ("this travelling madhouse") of an orchestra to have such credentials.

The standing ovation given to you and your marvellous music by that capacity Glasgow audience made me think while reading the Glasgow Herald on the following day, that their music critic, being probably the only person in the auditorium who didn't enjoy the evening, could have benefited from such a document but on the evidence of that review would find one hard to obtain.

LETTERS, LINES AND SPACES

There is a thin line in society between sanity and madness, is there not? Where many people find it difficult to accept the relatively mild maladjustments of a man who survived years of starvation and living hell only to discover that his entire family had been murdered for reasons of racial ideology, whilst the staple diet of entertainment for many western peoples now it seems, is violence, rape, murder and every imaginable depravity whether it is simulated on a Hollywood film set, or relayed live to the T.V. in a hotel bar.

Your music is hugely influential. I hope you know that. It restores some order, balance and faith in humanity in the lives of an awful lot of people.

In my early years, when I first played Elgar's The Music Makers with Adrian Boult, I read O'Shaughnessy's poem in the programme, and have never forgotten it. Since then I've sat by a few "desolate streams" in countless hotel rooms and aeroplane cabins, sometimes feeling that I'd lost the world that I had travelled through for most of my life, but your music reassures me of one thing at least. The world needs us: We ARE the "movers and shakers of the world forever it seems". I'm so looking forward to playing your "Requiem" and getting together again. I love to talk about the old youth orchestra days

I will be in Wales in early January for the Four Counties Youth Orchestra anniversary concert. They will be playing a piece of mine, which is a sort of trumpet concerto, dedicated to the great Willie Lang, who you may remember as the principal trumpet of the L.S.O. The soloist will be Huw Morgan who was,"B.B.C. Young Brass Player of the year 2005. I'm told he is quite brilliant and that he had asked specially to play the piece, having heard it at a concert in Austria despite never having heard of me or knowing that I was an ex member of the orchestra.

We will have a wonderful evening, I'm certain of that...Neil Kinnock will be presiding. He accepted the invitation with great excitement by return of post. Do you think you could manage to come? I'll let you have the exact date and venue when I get back to Edinburgh.

I will sleep now, that I feel tired at last, and in the absence of gunfire, thunderstorms or helicopters. Tomorrow we leave for Montevideo, and the last concert of the tour will be given in Buenos Aries.

We will play together soon again: and whatever happens Karin will be at the Cardiff concert Give our love to Carol and Jody.

Yours ever

Drac

LETTERS, LINES AND SPACES

Huw Morgan was BBC "Brass Player of the Year" in 2005

Huw Morgan
C/o Royal Academy of Music
Marylebone Road
London

Dear Huw

Thank you for your great playing of my piece in Cardiff. You really are a brilliant player and much more .The music sounded exactly as I had imagined it. I'm sure that, if I live to be a hundred I will never tire of the thrill and satisfaction of hearing my music presented with such care and enthusiasm. The amount of time, patience and effort invested by you and David and the orchestra was very obvious .It was a moving experience for me and more especially in the light of the occasion.

I'm on my way to Cardiff as I write. Train travel is perfect for relaxing and writing letters, and tonight I shall be playing at the Millennium Centre for the first time in a performance of "Cinderella" with Scottish Ballet. I've heard and read so much about the centre and I haven't played in Cardiff for many years --- I'm excited. As hell!

You were not able, from your dressing room, of course, to hear my pre-performance talk about "Y'r Wyddel" and afterwards it occurred to me that there might have been one or two things I hadn't told you about Willie Lang.

He played in Black Dyke band when he was still in short trousers which was when he made his famous recording of "Bless this House" for HMV, who referred to him on the cover as" Master William Lang" .The record sold two MILLION copies during the war.

If you have ever seen "A Man born to be King", that brilliant film based on a Rudyard Kipling story that stars Sean Connery and Michael Caine. You will remember the magical cornet playing over the beginning and end credits. Willie is the cornet player and the melody is "a minstrel boy to the war has gone." that was arranged for the film by Maurice Jarre. Those sessions were made very special by Willie's playing. I remember an atmosphere in the studio on the first day, when the cornet solo was recorded, that could never be described or repeated. All the music for that film was very much out of the ordinary. I was there to play the horn and various conch shells and animal horns. There were sitar players too, one of whom was the great Ravi Shankar and all kinds of drums, and drummers, with a lot of "ethnic" music that had to be improvised as you can imagine.

I watched the film again shortly after Willie's death. In December and all these memories came sadly but beautifully back.

When the story has been told and the film, nearly ended: there is a moment when Danny's crown, standing on the desk in Kipling's study, catches the lamplight and the minstrel boy and the cornet are heard for the last time. As I watched it, I thought of Willie and how he had gone to the war too, in Italy, as a tank driver in 1940. The story goes that he carried his cornet with him wherever he went.

I certainly never remember him being without it, and I will never forget the sound that he made with it.

Rain is splashing past the window now but the sun is breaking through up ahead and I shall be in Cardiff in an hour or so. Going back to Wales is always a great thrill for me.

It was a great pleasure to meet your parents. They were very obviously delighted that you are at the Academy now. You are side by side every day with the great and influential performers and composers of the future. In my time John Taverner and Michael Nyman recruited me for their first performances and Dame Eva Turner taught singing there. When she arrived in the morning and spoke to the hall porter you could hear her voice from the fourth floor landing.

LETTERS, LINES AND SPACES

Thank you again for your astounding playing. Your playing my music from memory especially touched me. That is a great privilege that maybe only composers can understand. I hope we can meet again very soon

Yours ever

Terry Johns

LETTERS, LINES AND SPACES

Lord Kinnock
House of Lords
Houses of Parliament
LONDON

17th January 2007

Dear Neil

I'm roasting by a big crackling fire, with the rain lashing at the windows. Life is normal again, that is to say I am able to spend some time with myself and write some letters.

The weekend was spent here at home – the calm punctuated by telephone calls from people still effervescent about the concert on Friday.

How can we thank you enough for coming and for your enthusiasm? Everyone I spoke to say that you had captured the spirit and tradition of youth and music in South Wales and expressed so perfectly in words what everyone was feeling. I will never forget it.

What a pity we didn't have more time to talk. I had so many things I wanted to say to you and to ask you.

Karin and I are in our eighteenth year in Edinburgh now. The city is home for her as you know and I still am fascinated by it. Many old friends visit me during the Festival, and when I can, I wander around the galleries and the old Georgian squares. It's a beautiful place to live.

I proudly conduct the Coop band in Glasgow now from time to time as associate conductor and write music for them. Like our concert, this is a full turn of the circle for me. I started playing at Tower Colliery band, when father was a young man and

LETTERS, LINES AND SPACES

working in the pit there. I blew my first note in that old engine shed and I've been blowing things ever since. It's still the first thing I do after breakfast.

We went to a band contest in November in the beautiful Scottish borders. A glorious day it was of autumn sunshine and blazing brass. The shops and pubs in the town all decorated with the colours of the bandsmen's uniforms. What gifts music gives us!

At the interval of our "Four Counties" concert, a horn player I had played with a long time ago came to see me. He brought his young son who has just started playing the horn, and who wanted to meet me because I had played at Darth Vader's funeral. Darth Vader's funeral, he assured me, was the defining moment in the history of the universe.

That concert was a defining moment for me and the boy's face said it all. It was like being back at Ogmore again, in the afternoon sunshine on the narrow path winding down to the sea.

Your being there made the evening for us all. The crowning moment being the singing at the end. So perfectly Welsh, and spontaneous like the choir on the bus, rattling up the valley from Ogmore to a concert.

I'll be in London in July for a Prom with the BBC Scottish. We'll be playing the ninth symphony of Mahler. Maybe you and Glenys would be free to come?

Thank you again.

Yours ever.

Drac

LETTERS, LINES AND SPACES

BILL LLOYD WAS A PRODUCER AT BBC SCOTLAND UNTIL 2009. IN THAT YEAR, CO-OP GLASGOW WON THE SCOTTISH BRASS BAND CHAMPIONSHIP FOR THE 29TH TIME, AND I COMPOSED A PIECE (GULL DANCES) FOR THEM, TO MARK THE OCCASION. IT WAS PLAYED AT A CONCERT IN EDINBURGH AND BILL PRODUCED THE BROADCAST FOR BBC RADIO SCOTLAND.

Bill Lloyd
C/o B.B.C. Scotland
City Hall
Glasgow

Dear Bill

Winter sunshine is glistening on the sea, and the sound of the waves is soothing me, slowly and gently after our week of blazing brass. The music is growing faint now in my imagination, like distant bells over the water, but it never goes far for long, and never has, since I was a boy. I write music, usually for brass, almost every morning now I am able to.

Mussels, leeks and parsley are simmering gently on the stove and the breeze from the sea is gently lifting the curtains. It's perfect here, in our little holiday home, that sits quietly under the trees and looks across the waters of the Forth, where postmen, retired publicans, and lorry drivers come, to relax. I like to walk by the shore in the evenings, where there is almost always someone with the same inclination, who will stop and talk for a while.

Thanks so much for all your work and patience at St.Cuthbert's. I hope you enjoyed the concert as much as we did. I listened to the broadcast on Sunday evening, and the radio sound did you credit; so warm and comfortable it was, like a log fire. It's obvious from the result, that you relish the sound of the band. They are amazing aren't they? There is a completely natural beauty and energy in brass band music that beguiled me when I was a young man, and gave me a desire for the musical life. As a boy I somehow by-passed the Rock and Roll revolution. I was too busy, I think, playing the cornet in the colliery band, whilst secretly trying to sound like Chet Baker. But the moment finally came when I decided against jazz as a means of making a living, which is why I'm now able to take regular meals and have warm clothes for the winter.

I was walking by the water on Sunday after the broadcast, thinking about St Cuthbert's beneath the castle, filled with the sound of brass, and weekend Edinburgh bubbling all around us, when it occurred to me that it was jazz that brought me here for the first time. When I was studying the horn at the Academy, I shared a flat with Henry Lowther and we used to go, two or three times a week, to Ronnie Scott's club in Gerrard St. which wasn't in the least bit posh or expensive in those days, and had a reduced entrance charge for students and M.U. members. Henry and I got our first gig together at the Edinburgh festival, in a dance revue" Collages", choreographed by Gillian Lynne with music by Dudley Moore. Edinburgh was fascinating to me then and has been ever

LETTERS, LINES AND SPACES

since. Every building was black with soot and there was a sweet smell of malt on the wind. We spent three weeks here that summer, and loved every minute, never imagining that I would get married here, or that it would be my home some day.

My fish stew asserts itself with the aroma of leeks and garlic and parsley, while the gulls are overhead screaming with what sounds like delighted anticipation. I shall be conducting band practice this evening and the sea will sing me to sleep.

I can't imagine life being any better than it is today Bill. Once again, profoundest thanks to you and the team for the broadcast and for your interest in my "hornography".

Best regards

Terry J

LETTERS, LINES AND SPACES

JOHN WILSON, THE CONDUCTOR AND ARRANGER GREATLY ADMIRED THE ORCHESTRAL PLAYING HE HEARD ON THE SOUNDTRACKS OF FILMS SUCH AS "OLIVER" AND "FIDDLER ON THE ROOF". FREELANCE (SESSION) PLAYING IN THE SIXTIES AND SEVENTIES IN LONDON WAS A LIFE THAT MANY MUSICIANS ASPIRED TO AS AN ALTERATIVE TO ORCHESTRAL PLAYING.

Waterfront Avenue
Edinburgh

Saturday morning

Dear John

Pale golden sunshine is on the sea this morning and the gulls are celebrating my retirement. Now that I don't have to live in hotels or play for money anymore, everything looks so different, and wide open, just like the Forth estuary beyond the balcony, where I sit writing almost every day now! Hearing your interest in these letters is very gratifying. You wrote in your message that you wanted to "know more" about the orchestra that played on the film of Oliver. Well – playing in that unique orchestra came almost at the beginning for me.

As a boy, while the rock revolution seemed to be changing everything so dramatically for everyone else, I was busy playing the cornet in the colliery band and trying, privately, to get a cool west coast jazz sound, in between Saturday mornings listening to the Ted Heath band on the BBC Home service.

I wanted more than anything, to be able to play jazz, so I learned dozens of standard tunes as time went on, mainly from playing the piano in pubs in the valleys for old colliers who changed key whenever they wanted to, which was marvellous aural training for me of course, although I didn't understand all that until much later.

LETTERS, LINES AND SPACES

Those famous names associated with Ted Heath became heroes to me, and the sound of that band was burned onto my musical memory for ever, so years later when I sat down at Denham to play my first session with Don Lusher, Kenny Baker, Eddie Blair and that huge orchestra, I really felt I had arrived, but with a mixture of feelings of nervousness, inadequacy and disbelief as they sat all around me, discussing the weather and the traffic! That was at Denham on the sound stage for the film of "Oliver" in 1968.

The end of the Heath band and the other big bands of that historic era brought so many of these great reed and brass players into the studios, and the string players were men, many of them Jewish, that had spent their earlier years playing in Walter Legge's Philharmonia, and Beecham's Royal Philharmonic. The sound the strings made has never been equalled, except possibly at Warner Bros, and the mix was perfect – definitive, for this kind of music. Besides the "Oliver" soundtrack you can hear that orchestra on the sound tracks of "Goodbye Mister Chips" 1969. "Scrooge" 1970, and "Fiddler on the Roof" from 1971.

(Isaac Stern recorded those famous opening credits with the producer trying to get him to sound like an old folk fiddler.).

"The Little Prince" came in 1974, with that exquisite orchestration by Angela Morley, and the "Slipper and the Rose", in 1976.

The orchestra recorded the film music of Korngold, Alfred Newman, and Bernard Herrmann too with Charles Gerhard for RCA Victor, the wind players for those recordings being drawn mostly from the London orchestras.

"Goodbye Mister Chips" was conducted by a young, almost unknown John Williams and it was at those sessions in London where I first met Nat Peck. Nat was a trombonist in the Glenn Miller band during the war and settled in Paris in 1945.

LETTERS, LINES AND SPACES

In the 70s and 80s Nat acted as contractor for a lot of people he had known and worked with in Paris, and brought many of them to London for recordings and films. Michel Legrand came to Olympic studios at Barnes to record an album with Barbara Streisand. Clark Terry made "Clark after dark" with a star-studded jazz orchestra conducted by Peter Herbholtzheimer at the same studio, and Phil Woods recorded "Images" at C.T.S. in Wembley. Philippe Sarde also came to London to record his film music, which was always full of jazz and Stan Getz came with him, as a featured player on two or three occasions. Heady days!

Nat put orchestras together for Lalo Schifrin's films, Sid Sax was the contractor for Jerry Fielding, Jerry Goldsmith, Henry Mancini, Elmer Bernstein, and Billy Goldenberg, and Sidney Margo handled the James Bond films for John Barry, so you can see what a great era it was for London studio players and as a french horn player, especially for me, being jazz educated so to speak. --- I was almost always invited.

In my early days, I toured Europe and America with symphony orchestras playing a concert almost every night, and I wasn't always as comfortable as I should have been with the music -- sometimes a huge symphony would pass in an instant, and after the final chord, would come that heart stopping silence, then the great wave of applause, that swept you to the safety of the shore.

Well! I'm here on dry land at last, exactly where I was meant to be, and I listen the sea as I go to sleep. Sometimes there's nothing to break the silence except the footsteps of the postman or a gull wandering home.

Thank you again John for being so enthusiastic and talented. There's a message to be delivered and you're the man to do it!

Very best regards

Terry

LETTERS, LINES AND SPACES

THE BEGINNING OF 2011 AND THE PERILOUS CONDITION OF THE WESTERN ECONOMY BROUGHT GREAT DIFFICULTIES TO ORCHESTRAS AND ARTS ORGANIZATIONS EVERYWHERE. IN THE USA, ORCHESTRAS HAD BEEN DEPENDENT FOR MANY YEARS ON PRIVATE DONATIONS, AND THE CONSEQUENCES OF THAT DEPENDENCE WERE BECOMING INCREASINGLY DIFFICULT IN TIMES OF ECONOMIC RESTRAINT. THERE WAS A WIDE DEBATE THAT WAS TAKING PLACE IN AMERICAN SOCIETY, AS TO THE IMPORTANCE OF THE "DIFFICULT" ARTS.

Detroit Symphony Orchestra   Waterfront Avenue
DETROIT   Edinburgh
Michigan   Scotland

28th February 2011

Dear Friends

We are nearly in the month of March and near the end of the long Scottish winter. The snow, wind and rain from the Forth estuary, have been growling and moaning outside my window for months. This morning, sunlight filled the room as I opened the door, and the breeze from the sea, gently lifted the curtains and my spirits. I don't take part in the rough and tumble of orchestral life any more but your predicament is, of course, a familiar one that is becoming more widespread in these troubled times.

When I was a young man, I travelled with a chamber group to give a concert in a village in one of the affluent southern counties of England. Having finished our afternoon rehearsal, we all went into the church hall for a pre-concert meal that was meant to have been organised by the local music club. The trestle tables were bare and the room was empty except for a dramatic scene that was being enacted in the corner, in which the central tragic character was a lady, in cashmere, pearls, and considerable distress, who was being attended to, and consoled, by a small group of people. Eventually her incoherence, and anxiety to communicate the reasons for her disquiet, culminated in the loud anguished cry, " But what sort of food do musicians eat!"

This hapless lady, sobbing and squeezing her sodden handkerchief in the heart of rural England, had been too frightened and bewildered to perform the relatively simple task allotted to her, of providing food for us, apparently because it would have involved some understanding of the mysterious and unknown dietary requirements of itinerant musicians.

Mistrust and semi anonymity have been constant companions in our countless disputes with managers, critics and agents for many years here in Britain.

At one point in the sixties, the Royal Philharmonic orchestra officially did not exist, having been excluded from performing at the Royal Festival Hall and deprived of its Royal status. On the death of Sir Thomas Beecham the RPO's players were informed that they were not entitled to any benefit from his musical legacy, and that the orchestra should disband. The British Arts Council, the Royal Philharmonic Society, the music critics of the London newspapers, the heads of the major record companies, and the international agents were by and large in agreement with that view.

That was the beginning of a long winter for us, and there were to be many more to come, and I was reminded yesterday of those unhappy times, whilst reading about your current and depressingly familiar travails. Our enemies did retreat eventually, but that did not happen without a protracted struggle accompanied by a torrent of libel, slander and antagonism that was directed at us as a penalty for daring to ask for some degree of control over our own lives.

During one newspaper exchange about players' salaries, a retired army major from Cirencester was infuriated to discover that orchestral musicians got paid AT ALL! and somehow managed to connect the whole thing with the battle of El Alamein! But embattled as we were then, that eminent orchestra is now still very much in existence as you will know, and entertains the public of most countries of the World to this day, having control of its own affairs under the guidance of a board of directors, elected from and by the orchestral players themselves. This is of course, by no means a perfect system, but it offers the players SOME degree of autonomy. How else can music be made?

> We are the music makers
> And we are the dreamers of dreams,
> Wandering by lone sea-breakers,
> And sitting by desolate streams; -
> World losers and world-forsakers,
> On whom the pale moon gleams:
> Yet we are the movers and shakers
> Of the world forever, it seems.

The doors and windows are wide open to the sea. The sun is shining at last, and the gulls are cheering you all on to victory.

Very best wishes, huge admiration and good luck.

Terry Johns

P.S Every orchestra here in Britain, has at one time or another in its history been crippled by the excessive fees charged by conductors, agents, and management, and they have been threatened, cheated, misrepresented or lied to, but I can only say that for myself this has been a small price to pay for the glittering gift that I was given.

LETTERS, LINES AND SPACES

But we, with our dreaming and singing,

Ceaseless and sorrowless we!

The glory about us clinging

Of the glorious futures we see

Our souls with high music ringing:

O men it must ever be

That we dwell, in our dreaming and singing,

A little apart from ye.

Printed in Great Britain
by Amazon

12178690R00098